JUST YOU, JUST ME

Erika sat silently. Judy was sulking again.

"Dammit, you always do this to me. The minute my back is turned you let another girl . . ."

"But we never . . ."

"Makes no difference. If you cared about me at all, you'd have waited for me to come home," Judy snapped, the folds of her fragile nightgown coming loose as she paced around the tiny bedroom.

Erika said nothing. She didn't want to desire Judy now. She didn't even like her at these moments. But her need was stronger than her anger as her eyes travelled to a bare spot on Judy's shoulder. The need became irresistible. "Let's not talk now," she purred.

Judy's hand shot out. The slap was so unexpected that Erika didn't feel it for a moment. Before she could reply, she saw tears come into Judy's eyes and the tall, sensual girl gathered her in her arms. There was a faint rustle of silk against nylon.

"Don't you love me anymore?" Judy sobbed.

"You know I do."

Judy began to unbutton Erika's blouse with shaking fingers. "Then love me. Right here. Never mind the bed, just show me you love me."

JOURNEY TO FULFILLMENT

by Valerie Taylor

A VOLUTE BOOK

1982

Printed in the United States of America

Cover design and photograph of the author by Tee A. Corinne

ISBN: 0-930044-31-2

JOURNEY TO FULFILLMENT
was first published in 1964

A VOLUTE BOOK

published by
THE NAIAD PRESS, INC.
P.O. Box 10543
Tallahassee, Florida 32302

Other VOLUTE BOOKS by Valerie Taylor

A WORLD WITHOUT MEN
RETURN TO LESBOS

The imprint, A VOLUTE BOOK, tells the reader she is reading a classic Lesbian novel from the past, reprinted in a paperback edition. THE NAIAD PRESS proudly begins this new series with three of Valerie Taylor's major Lesbian novels from the 1960s.

CHAPTER ONE

THERE WAS no fence around the Children's Resettlement Camp. That was the first thing Erika saw as the jeep jolted to a stop in front of it. The low, unpainted buildings had been set down like dollhouses on a grassy flat space, behind them, snow-topped mountains towered against a blue and sunny sky. No fences anywhere.

"Die Alpen," Erika whispered. She felt pleased with herself for recognizing them. Out of some other life, the small black and white photograph set among columns of print, the summer sky full of soft, white clouds. The camp buildings were new, but the peaks in the background were familiar. Alps.

She looked around. No fences, no guards, no one in uniform except the man at whose side she sat, and his pockets bulged with candy bars and bubble gum.

He looked relieved as Miss Campbell came running across the open space the way she always did, as though the new children were her very own and they had been separated by time and space and nameless perils. Reminded him of his first grade teacher, for all her English accent. He said, "Four of 'em this time, Miss Campbell. The little ones been raising hell the whole way, guess they thought I was going to fry them for breakfast. But this girl's been a perfect lady."

He patted Erika's shoulder. She sat stiff and unmoving, but a flicker of fear crossed her face. His hand dropped.

Miss Campbell said, "It's the uniform. All uniforms mean the same thing to them." She switched to

7

a stiff classroom German, raising her voice. "Come on, children. Dinner is waiting for you, with milk. Milk from America!"

The sergeant boosted the children to the ground. The smallest one screamed. He patted her head, newly shaven to get rid of the lice and already sprouting new blonde fuzz. "They'll be cute when you get a little meat on their bones," he said, making his voice tough because every new load of kids from the camps made him choke up. The ones they had found among the piles of dead hadn't been much thinner. He added, "My wife sent some new pictures of the baby. She's starting to walk now."

"She must be beautiful. Let me see them before you start back." Miss Campbell picked up the little one and started patting her in an accustomed way, but her eyes were on Erika. It was the quiet children who had trouble adjusting. The little ones would be yelling happily on the playground in a day or two, but the teenagers broke down six months, a year, maybe ten years later—time would show how deep the wounds were. She said in her high clear voice, *"Komm', komm'! Essen!"*

Erika was used to obeying. She jumped down from the jeep and stepped into the big open space, still looking around, uneasy because everything was strange, but careful to keep a space between herself and the man. The nausea that his touch aroused in her was ebbing away. She reminded herself that it was daylight and outdoors, and that the woman was in charge here, not just a tool of the officers as the female camp guards had been.

Here there were no guards, no one in uniform at all. She followed Miss Campbell and the American soldier into the largest building, through a room thinly furnished with plain chairs and tables and dominated by a big desk covered with papers. The

8

next room was larger still and had an old-fashioned cookstove at one end, beyond long plank tables and backless wooden benches. Erika had never seen such a stove before. And it was a long time since she had seen a woman as plump and comfortable looking as the one who stood beside it, smiling, her chubby figure swathed in a checked apron.

Two big girls in blue jeans and sweaters stood filling bowls from a big kettle on the back of the stove. Thick braids swung as they moved. They looked at Erika and the three little ones, sizing them up. One of them had a long healed scar that ran down the side of her face from eye to chin. Erika's hand flew up to hide her own scar. Her shirtsleeve slipped back, too big for the thin wrist, and the row of purple numerals on her forearm showed. She pulled the cuff down quickly.

The girl smiled. She brought Erika the first bowl, walking past the expectant little children. Her fingers touched Erika's lightly as she set it down. This time Erika didn't shrink away. She took the bowl and stood holding it, not sure what to do. The soup smelled of onions and meat—actually meat!—but the thought of eating made her stomach cramp. The candy bar the soldier had given her on that endless ride felt heavy in her; she could still taste its too rich sweetness.

The little girls ate noisily. She sat down beside them and bent her head over her bowl. Miss Campbell was pouring milk from a big shiny pitcher into bright, plastic mugs. Apparently in this place the bosses worked too. Erika's timidity deepened. She didn't know how to behave or what to expect.

She felt tired and confused. So much had happened in the two weeks since the American tanks and trucks rolled into the prison camp, loaded with G. I.'s who didn't look like soldiers even though they

9

wore uniforms, and bringing food, cigarettes, blankets—things nobody could believe still existed. It was hard enough to believe there was still a world beyond the camp, outside the fences.

She had moved through the sights and sounds of the liberation like a sleepwalker, only stirred to the familiar dread when one of the soldiers came too near. They treated her exactly as they did the little children. She supposed the things that had happened to her in the last three years didn't show on her face, and there was nothing adult about her flat chest and skinny arms and legs. But the reflex was beyond her control. When a man got close enough for her to feel his body heat or smell the male odor, she began to shake.

Now time had come to a stop and she was sitting beside a long bare table, eating soup without tasting it. It was like waking after a long monotonous dream. The real world was still out of focus.

She looked at Miss Campbell, a woman from another world; then at her bowl. The soup steamed gently. There were pieces of meat in it. Suddenly she was ravenous. She gulped it quickly, turning up the bowl to get the last drops. The girl with the scarred cheek took the bowl out of her hands and took it to the stove to refill it. It was as though she had been waiting for that hungry look, expecting it, even hoping for it. She smiled proudly as she set the second serving down in front of Erika.

As if she could read my mind, Erika thought in wonder. Her spoon moved mechanically—her mind was on the girl.

Miss Campbell said, "Katja, Erika will sleep in the big girls' cabin, in the bed Lisabet had. Show her where it is, please, and then bring her to Number Six for clothes."

She was used to obeying. She got up, heavy with

10

sleep and food, and followed Katja out of the eating-cooking room.

The two girls crossed the open space in front of the building. The grass felt strange under Erika's heavy boots. She walked carefully, trying to look at Katja without attracting her attention. But Katja caught the look and gave her a good-natured grin.

"You'll sleep next to me. It was Lisabet's bed, but now she's gone to South America. The Red Cross found her aunt in Venezuela. Do you have a family anywhere?"

"Mine are all dead." She hadn't really thought about them for a long time; she was more interested in the other girl's accent. "What part of Germany are you from?"

"Me? I'm a Pole. There are a lot of us in this place, and other nationalities too. We all speak German though, it's the only way to understand everybody. I was at Oranienberg." She added casually, "They hit us on the face there too, for punishment. Ten lashes with a belt buckle. Where were you?"

"A little place called Steinhagen."

Both of them took prison for granted, it had been their childhood world, but Katja had been away from it longer. She had been liberated in the first days of the American invasion. So far, Erika hadn't had a chance to wonder what would happen next or how the new life would differ from the old. She nodded, not thinking about the gas ovens or the crematoria but about Katja's voice, which was cheerful and pleasant in spite of, or because of, her funny accent. The two girls smiled at each other.

Katja led the way past several of the long, low barracks and stopped in front of one, well toward the back of the camp. She pulled the door open and led the newcomer into a large bare room with two rows of army cots. "Here. This is your bed." It was covered

11

with a G.I. blanket. Erika stood looking at it, unable to believe that it had anything to do with her.

"I know how you feel. It's like that for all of us at first. You have to forget all that, you know."

Erika said, troubled, "Nothing seems real."

"I know." Katja stood looking at her. She was a big-boned girl with a bosom that filled out her khaki sweater. She caught Erika's look and grinned. "Lord, it's hot in here." She pulled off the sweater and unfastened the top button of her shirt. A deep shadowed hollow showed at the base of her throat; the suntan ended abruptly and the skin below was soft and white. To her own surprise, Erika wanted to unfasten the next button and touch that smooth whiteness. She looked away.

Katja smiled. She had a broad face with high cheekbones; her smile was wide and warm. "You'll feel all right in a few days. Do you have dreams? Wake me if you have. I used to scream murder at night when I first came here, but now I sleep all night long."

"I don't know," Erika said dully. She stood in the narrow aisle between the double rows of beds, her arms hanging down, feeling lonely and lost.

Katja nodded. She put her arms around Erika's shoulders and hugged her gently, as she might have hugged a new baby. "What little skinny bones you have. Anyway, they'll feed you up here. Food parcels from America and everything. How old are you, anyhow? You haven't got much chest yet."

"Almost sixteen."

"I'm seventeen. Lisabet looked like you, a little. Blonde hair and big gray eyes. She was my best chum."

Erika wished miserably that she could be Katja's best chum, but she didn't know how to say so. She sighed, standing in the careful embrace of the larger and older girl.

Katja kissed her. It was a long time since she had been kissed; the gesture belonged to the forgotten time when she had had a family. The men whose heavy bodies had smothered her hadn't kissed her. One or two had slapped her, afterwards, when their uniforms were buttoned up again and they had no more use for her.

She couldn't clearly remember any kiss, but she knew that Katja's was different from, say, her mother's. She wished it could last forever. She wanted much more. What, she didn't know, but all the feeling in her seemed to have come to life and flowed into her mouth. She was afraid to breathe.

The door creaked. Katja stepped back, letting her go. She said loudly, "Come on, let's go and get you some clothes. Then we'll find the other big girls. You're my best chum though, aren't you?"

They went out into the open space. It didn't seem so big now. The mountains were still there, huge and cold, but she wasn't so afraid of them. Katja put an arm through hers and hugged her close. Her body was warm and solid.

Erika felt safe for the first time since the G.I.'s had opened the prison gates. She let herself be led across the springy grass, between the buildings, with the other girl's warm hand on her arm. Tonight or tomorrow she might be numb again, but for the time being she felt warm and hopeful.

CHAPTER TWO

THE EARLY mornings were cool even in summer. Erika hugged her arms across her chest for warmth as she stood looking down the mountain road. The smaller children were running to meet the supply truck, although it was at least a mile away; in this thin, clear air, things looked closer than they actually were. Erika still felt that she ought to be able to reach out and touch the mountains, but Miss Campbell said it would take half a day's walking even to reach the foothills.

Miss Campbell joined them carrying the newest little boy, a rack of bones who looked two years old and was five. He kept his face buried in her neck. One of the big boys said wisely, "He's afraid." Miss Campbell said, "Only for a little while. It's good for him to be with the others." The little boy peeked into her face and then shut his eyes again.

It was a strange thing, Erika thought. Here they all were in Switzerland, a country that didn't have dictators or wars. Kids from all over the world, Germany and Austria, Poland, Czechoslovakia, Holland, Hungary. All living together and speaking German, more or less. And here was this American army truck bringing food and clothes and blankets and soap from the Red Cross, to be distributed by an English schoolteacher, two American Quakers and a round-faced lady from Latvia.

And mail. Letters from all over the world, some of them from relatives the children dimly remembered or had never heard of before. Thaddeus was waiting for a money order to pay his way to Chicago

14

—his aunt wrote that there were a lot of Polish people in Chicago. And Channah would go to Hong Kong where her uncle owned a store, as soon as the English would let her in.

But she, Erika, had nobody. Her father and Uncle David had been taken into "protective custody" soon after the *Anschluss*. And she had come home from the food distribution center to find the rest of the family machine-gunned, frozen to the sidewalk by their own blood. Mutti and little Kurt and Tante Lise.

She was alone. In the whole world nobody belonged to her. Except maybe Katja, who reached across the space between their cots at night and held her hand. Kissing, holding hands, they both wanted much more than that with each other. Erika wasn't sure what she wanted or how it could be had, in a place where there were always people around, but Katja's touch left her frustrated and hungry.

As if she had been thinking the same thought, Katja moved ahead and stood beside her. They stood watching the advance of the truck, the high point of everyone's week.

Katja indicated Miss Campbell with a twitch of the elbow. "She's been writing letters about you. I saw the carbons on her desk."

"In her desk, you mean."

"All right, it's her own fault if she doesn't lock things away safely. She's been writing to someone in America about you."

"But I don't know anybody in America!"

"Shut up, can't you!" Katja looked around. "Sometimes people adopt children. Rich people. Maybe a rich family will adopt you."

Erika considered this. America didn't seem like a real place to her, although much of the canned food

15

supplied by the Red Cross came from there and Miss Campbell had shown it to them on the globe. All she knew about it was that everyone had a lot of money and everything was done by electrical appliances. She couldn't imagine living in such a fairyland country. "Oh, you're making it up. Why would anyone adopt me?"

"Because you're so cute. Who knows why Americans do anything, anyhow? They're all rich."

"Then I hope they've sent us some chocolate bars." She pulled Katja closer as the truck rounded the last curve and started up the home stretch to the camp. About half of the other children, including a few from the big boys' barracks, rushed to meet it.

Erika had come to like the camp routine, the order and the feeling of belonging. In the afternoon there was school-work and play and more work. After the inertia of the camp it felt good to be in a place where everyone had something to do.

In the seven weeks since her arrival Erika had washed dishes, peeled vegetables, scrubbed clothes on an old-fashioned board and hung them out in the clean air to dry. She and Katja took care of their barracks, hurrying through the sweeping so they could touch each other for a minute. It was their only chance to be alone. They would look at each other across the supper table with the same daydreams in their eyes.

Today she helped put away the food. That was fun, not work.

Erika realized that it was past time for her English class, but no one seemed to care. She wasn't interested in learning English, she didn't know anyone in the countries where it was spoken, but Miss Campbell was insistent. Today, though, Miss Campbell was reading her mail. On truck days everything was different.

Miss Campbell came to the door and watched them for a moment. Then she said in her usual calm tone, "Erika, please come with me. I want to speak with you."

Had she found out about Katja? Erika put down the box of rice and followed her into the office. She stood beside the desk until Miss Campbell said absently, "Sit down, why don't you?" and indicated the straight chair that was kept for visitors and discipline cases. Erika was afraid to guess what was coming.

"How would you like to go to America?"

"But I have no family! I don't know anyone in America!"

Miss Campbell found the letter she was looking for and spread it open, looking rather like the harassed school principal which she had once been. She said, "I have a cousin who married an American. They live in Illinois, near Chicago, in a suburb called Worthington. Their daughter is a student at Northwestern University." She put down the envelope and looked at Erika. "They want you to come and live with them until you are through school."

"But why? *Warum?*" Why, she wondered, would these people take a stranger into their home, especially since they already had a daughter? She said, "A boy I can understand, if they have a girl already. But why me?"

"Maybe because you're the right age to be Judy's little sister. Maybe they feel the war has passed them by." She sounded a little unkind, remembering London under the V-1 bombs and the safety her cousin had enjoyed in the States. "Have you any objection to going?"

"Oh, no. What else is there for me to do?"

Miss Campbell smiled. "Only time will tell. But you must be the one to decide."

"I want to go."

"It will take a few weeks. You've had your physical checkup, there's nothing wrong except the weight. Our office in Zurich will take care of the legal papers. In the meantime you must study your English lessons. We'll find proper clothes for the trip. Lucy will want to outfit you for school." She smiled. "You can have a good life. Do your part by growing up well."

"Yes, sure. Thank you."

But she wasn't listening. She sat wide-eyed. Miss Campbell said, "That's all. You can tell the others if you like."

They were still unpacking. All but Katja, who put down a tin and came to meet her. Erika said, "Come on." They walked out of the kitchen together, not caring what the others thought.

The big girls' cabin was empty and neat. Erika pulled the door shut behind them. There was no lock, but it would creak if anyone tried to open it. "You know what? I'm going to America!"

"I told you so. Are you sure?"

"Yes, to Campbell's relatives."

"She's English, stupid."

"Just the same, she has some cousin married to a rich American. Their daughter is at the University."

Katja said fiercely, "You better not like her. You better not like anybody but me."

"I won't."

For an instant she thought Katja was going to cry. Nobody in Children's Camp ever cried, except the very small ones who hadn't learned that crying did no good. Now here was Katja with her face puckering, rubbing a hand across her eyes. Erika asked curiously, "Did you cry when Lisabet went away?"

"Goddam it, I'm not crying."

"I know it. I was just asking."

Katja said roughly, "Shut up and put your hand

18

here." She unbuttoned her G.I. shirt. There was nothing under it but flesh, soft and smooth. Her breasts were full and round with dark red buds, what Erika called "buttons." She touched one. It stood up hard and eager. Katja said hoarsely, "Go ahead, kiss me." Erika cupped both hands around the milky-white globes. They were soft yet solid, smooth yet heavy.

Her lips closed over a tight red bud. Excitement flooded her entire body, centering in the place she tried not to think about; the place the soldiers had violated. But this was different. This was what she had wanted all the time, not knowing what it was she longed for when she lay awake and looked at Katja's face in the moonlight. Her breath quickened.

Katja moaned softly.

Neither of them cared at that moment whether they were caught or not.

Both of them had forgotten about America. Even the shadow of separation could not come between them now.

CHAPTER THREE

"SEAT BELT buckled?" The stewardess bent to check, smiling maternally at the white-faced little girl in the navy beret. "Are you flying all the way to New York? How exciting!"

She seemed to expect an answer, but Erika didn't know what to say. She muttered, "Yes," and left it there. The stewardess asked, "Would you like some chewing gum? It keeps your ears from popping as we go up. Or a magazine to read?"

"No, thanks." Erika sat stiffly upright, watching her as she moved to the man across the aisle, a Swiss business type who had already unstrapped his briefcase and taken out a sheaf of dull-looking papers. In her trim uniform the girl looked young and poised, but impersonal. There was no one else under forty on board.

There was a whirring sound and a vibration. Erika realized that they were about to take off. She felt excited, frightened and a little sick. She folded her hands in her lap and waited. Since she had the window seat, she could see Miss Campbell standing in a little crowd of people just inside the barrier. She wasn't waving, she just stood there with her face turned toward the departing plane, smiling.

Erika had been sorry when Miss Campbell told her the trip would be made by plane. In her childhood —the lost childhood out of which thoughts and memories were reviving with increasing frequency —she had dreamed about crossing the ocean on a ship. She had never seen an ocean liner outside the pages of magazines, but she had a clear picture in her mind of the one she would take, and for the first few days after Miss Campbell's astonishing news she had imagined herself on the aft deck, looking at the endless gray waves as they rolled away behind the ship.

She was disappointed to learn that she would fly from Zurich with a short stopover in Ireland. It made a life-changing journey seem trivial somehow, like taking a bus to the market.

But the American Campbells were paying for her ticket. She accepted it as she had accepted everything in the last three years: hunger and abuse, combat boots, bubble gum, English lessons. In prison you learn to take what comes without too much excitement, glad when it's good, sorry when it's bad and always aware that things will change sooner or later, for better or worse. If she had to fly, she would fly. If the plane crashed—too bad.

The one thing that hurt was leaving Katja. She tried not to think about it. They never mentioned it —their talk was all about America—but the few minutes of privacy they managed to find were filled with new intensity. The realization that she would never see Katja again was like being stabbed by a small sharp blade, a momentary pain but a sharp one. At the same time she was comforted by a realization that shamed her while it consoled. She never admitted it in so many words, even to herself. But it was there.

Somewhere in the world there were other girls like Katja.

Katja had known Lisabet, and others before her. Then there must be many girls, perhaps even in America, who knew about their way of kissing and touching. And more. She wasn't sure what "more" in-

21

volved, but she felt sure it went beyond her delight in Katja's bosom and the hungry pressure of their two bodies when they stole a moment alone. The experiments they dared stirred so great a hunger in her that she felt instinctively there must be a satisfaction for it, just as there was when she hungered for food. She decided that if they had a bed and a door that locked, without danger of interruption, they could find out. But such privacy wasn't forthcoming in Children's Camp.

At the end there was no chance to say a private good-bye. She shook hands with everyone, counsellors and children alike, before getting into the truck with Miss Campbell and Sergeant Rivers. Katja's plump work-rough fingers held hers for a moment. She looked into a pair of tear-filled eyes. For a moment she had a wild impulse to throw her arms around Katja and scream that she wasn't going. Then the hand dropped hers, and someone else took her cold fingers.

Now she leaned back in her seat with the belt fastened snugly around her waist and relaxed, looking neither back nor ahead. The future was still formless. She had no material from which to build a picture, except the illustrations in Brad's American magazines. The past was gone. There was only this time of transit.

The noise of the motors deepened and steadied. Then, unbelievably, they were rolling across the field, still on the ground but actually moving. She could no longer see Miss Campbell. She realized that until this moment she hadn't actually believed she was going. Now her world lay inside this big transatlantic airliner, cut off from the sixteen years before, not yet connected with the years to come.

It was her last attempt to think ahead until they

22

landed to refuel at Gander. She sat looking at the soft white clouds as they gained altitude, and then at the other passengers. Nothing existed except the present.

CHAPTER FOUR

"WE'RE COMING IN. That's the Statue of Liberty."

It was a gray shape in the fog. Erika glanced at it and then at the skyline. Tall, windowed, inhuman, the buildings of downtown New York rose into a gray rain-threatening sky. Here and there were blobs of green, like chunks of sponge rubber, which she realized were parks. It seemed incredible that anything could grow here, that people could live here.

The stewardess said, "It's beautiful on a clear day. The airport is outside the city, but you can see quite a lot as we come in." But why should a Swiss girl be so defensive about New York City? Proud to be on this important flight, perhaps.

Erika was afraid she was going to be sick. She didn't know whether it was the coffee she had been served with lunch or the way the plane bumped and jolted as it lost altitude, as though there were ruts in the air. Her ears crackled alarmingly. She shut her eyes, hoping she might feel better if she didn't have to look at the tilting buildings.

The man across the aisle said in his heavy Swiss German, "Open your mouth. It equalizes the pressure."

She didn't know what he meant, but she had no intention of landing with her mouth open, like an idiot. She put her fingers in her ears and sat stiffly erect, feeling that if they landed safely she would never leave the ground again.

There was a small bump, much less noticeable than the ones they had been feeling, but different. Erika opened her eyes and saw that they were taxiing along a vast plane of concrete between two rows of colored lights. She felt bewildered and tired, much as she had felt on the day of liberation. And her knees and back ached from sitting still so long.

The airport was like a city, building after building reaching as far as she could see in the misty air. At their gate fifty or sixty people were waiting. Except for her.

Terror shook her. Suppose Mr. and Mrs. Miller didn't meet her? Suppose they had changed their minds? No, that was foolish. But suppose they had an accident on the way to the airport? She was alone in a foreign country with five dollars, one small suitcase and a scanty store of English of which, at this moment, she couldn't remember one word.

What would she do if nobody came for her?

She looked around, but there was no one she recognized, not even one of her fellow passengers. She was lost in a whirlpool of reunited families.

"You are Erika Frohmann?"

She had been looking for a replica of Miss Campbell. The woman in front of her looked much younger, yet it was easy to tell, somehow, that she wasn't as young as she looked. She had a slender figure, well girdled and uplifted; expert makeup; neat curls under a pillbox hat. She wore a simple sleeveless dress that no middle-aged European woman would have worn on the street, smart shoes with high heels, jewelry—bracelet, wristwatch, lapel pin, glasses with silver-patterned frames.

But those were Miss Campbell's calm gray eyes behind the odd-shaped lenses. Relief washed over Erika. The voice went on, "I am Lucy Miller. Come with me, my husband waits for us."

She took Erika's case and pushed the door open to let her go first into the building. In the long echoing hall she looked around, then lapsed into English.

"Is this all you have? Good, Carl will get you through Customs in no time. We'll have plenty of time to fit you out for school, the semester doesn't begin for almost six weeks. I do hope you're going to be happy with us."

Erika said, "Yes," wondering what she was agreeing to. Only the last sentence made sense; the rest was too fast and too full of unfamiliar words. Superimposed on the clear crisp speech which must originally have been like Miss Campbell's was a blurry accent that reminded her of Sergeant Rivers. It was impossible to follow.

Anyway, she reminded herself, now she would have food and a place to sleep. This woman had a kind face. And all the people here looked so well fed, wore such good (if astonishingly informal) clothes, seemed to move as though they had always had plenty of everything. It was reassuring.

Mr. Miller, waiting for them under "F" in Customs, didn't seem to have much to say in any language. He gave her a warm smile and a fatherly pat on the shoulder, and opened her little case for the Customs officer. She watched him while the official went through her things. He looked about forty-five, which was probably his wife's age too; he too wore glasses, and his shirt had short sleeves and hung out over his trousers. His was the forty-five of a man who has always had plenty of good nourishing food, plenty of milk on cold nights; a man to whom the drone of a plane overhead means only the morning mail. Erika had known much younger men who were breathing cadavers, wrinkled and gray-haired, moving painfully on rheumatic legs like knobbed sticks.

America, she thought gratefully.

She was silent during the taxi ride to the hotel, looking out of the window at grimy warehouses and then at open streets with brisk crowds and shiny cars moving bumper to bumper. At their hotel she followed the older couple in and was silently terrified as they were whisked up to the fourteenth floor, which was directly above the twelfth. She tried to get her breath back while Mr. Miller tapped at a closed door, then pushed it open.

It was a large, pleasantly impersonal hotel bedroom with half-packed suitcases lying around—and the most beautiful girl she had ever seen bending over the bed, folding dresses. She was slender but healthy-looking, with reddish brown hair in a glossy, long bob, dark blue eyes, and a smooth suntan. She wore the shortest and whitest shorts Erika had ever seen, even in a magazine illustration, dazzling against her brown thighs, and a narrow halter that let her breasts all but spill free over the cleverly seamed cloth. The sight embarrassed Erika and made her feel a little faint. But the middle-aged parents seemed to take this near-nudity for granted.

"Judy, Erika's here. The plane got in on schedule."

Judy said, "Hi." She folded a lacy slip with deft hands (bright rose polish on oval nails and a charm bracelet jingling with gold trifles) and laid it in the suitcase before she bothered to look up. It was impossible to tell what she thought about Erika. She asked as a polite afterthought, "Have a nice trip?"

"Yes, thank you."

"Planes are fun, don't you think? I'm flying to France next year for my Junior Year. It'll be super."

About three-fourths of this meant nothing to Erika; some of the words were familiar but they didn't seem to go together. But she gathered that the intention was friendly, and gave Judy her small, unsure smile. There was a short, strained silence.

She had seen women, both living and dead, with no rag of clothing. But they were skin and bones, with the impersonality that suffering gives. The sol-

27

diers who had used her were inextricably associated with their harsh gray-green uniforms. Katja, the first person to stir her senses, meant touch rather than sight, warmth and excitement more than a visual image.

Now, only a few feet away, under the strong electric light and the affectionate eyes of her parents, was a healthy young girl dressed only in two strips of cloth that left little to the imagination. Erika tried not to look where the thin fabric wrinkled between her thighs or the shadowed hollow at the base of her neck. The feelings Katja had waked in her were stirring again.

She wondered if it were a custom in America to go around half-naked. True, the suntan made it seem less personal. But she was afraid to look too closely, in case her feelings showed in her face. The narrow halter, hiding so little, was more provocative than actual nakedness would have been.

Mrs. Miller picked a pajama jacket off the bed and folded it, somewhat absently. "It's going to be a hot day now that the sun's coming out. Even the Middle West is nothing compared to New York in summer. I don't suppose you have anything cooler to put on?" She looked dubiously at Erika's little suitcase, which seemed to shrink under her eyes.

"I am sorry, I have nothing."

Judy said, "I'll find you something."

"Your things will be too big for her, dear."

"Maybe a gathered skirt and peasant blouse? Anyhow she won't absolutely melt in them."

Carl Miller said kindly, "You girls fix it up between you. Only don't take all day getting dressed, because I'm hungry and we have to make a plane of four-thirty."

They are so kind, Erika thought, and there is so much they don't know. She was tired, and not hungry at all; she felt heavy and stuffy from the tray lunch on the plane, and now it seemed that she was expected to eat again. She would have liked to lie down on that big smooth bed and go to sleep, but she felt it would be rude to say so.

Mrs. Miller was right about one thing; it was hot. Perspiration trickled down her back under the heavy serge jacket, which she hadn't thought of taking off. She stood uncertainly as the grownups drifted out of the room. She could hear their key in the lock next door. This then was Judy's room; this was where she had slept the night before. There was a pang in the thought of Judy curled up in bed.

Judy said, "I'm sorry I can't speak one word of German. I'm doing a minor in French because I'll be in Paris next year—that's right, I told you that. Why don't you take a shower while I find you something to put on?" She sounded pleasant and kind, like a teacher.

Because gestures accompanied it, Erika understood this. She let herself be shown into a bathroom like the ones she had seen in Brad's magazines but never quite believed in. Judy closed the door behind her, leaving her alone with the baffling faucets and mixers.

Only yesterday she would have been overwhelmed by all this luxury: the thick pastel towels, fat bars of soap, the row of jars and boxes Judy had lined up on the glass shelf over the basin. Now, as she stood under a too-cool torrent she didn't know how to regulate, covering herself with lather from a gorgeously perfumed bar of pink soap, she was thinking about the girl on the other side of the door.

She could hear Judy walking around, pulling out drawers, taking things off hangers, making the small intimate sounds of a woman changing her clothes.

The bathroom door opened without warning. Erika froze, trying to hide behind her hands. Judy

29

dropped an armful of light-colored garments on the hamper. "Try these for size. You finding everything you need?"

She had changed to a sleeveless dress and slippers with heels; her lips were made up and her hair arranged. That Erika was both naked and embarrassed didn't seem to bother her. She gave her another of those friendly impersonal smiles and withdrew, closing the door upon a nervous and frightened Erika.

But I am not so terribly ugly, she reminded herself. In fact, my body is quite all right. She wasn't sure why it mattered. But she knew that in this country, so big and bright and fast-moving, she had already found someone to admire. Even if Judy saw her only as a child in need of kindness, recipient of an impersonal generosity, she could feel this secret longing whenever they were together in the same room. No one would know.

She rubbed herself dry with a big pink towel, hardly noticing its thickness and softness because she was remembering Judy's smile.

CHAPTER FIVE

"WHAT'S THE matter?"

Erika looked in bewilderment from Judy to the pile of clothes on her bed. "Please, you are going away?"

"Oh, that!" Judy showed her strong, white teeth in a smile. "I'm going to be a camp counsellor. You know, camp. In the woods."

From Erika's baffled expression it was plain that she didn't know what a camp counsellor was. "Like Aunt Ellen, sort of."

"You have here children without parents, also?"

"No, they go camping for fun. Their parents pay for it. And how!"

That didn't make sense either. Erika hovered in the doorway, not sure whether to come in or stay out. In this friendly household people simply knocked and then, with or without an invitation, walked in. There were no locks such as she remembered from her own childhood. And no one seemed to mind having people around all the time.

Judy said politely, "Come in, why don't you?" She was folding shirts and shorts, of which she seemed to have an endless supply, and stacking them in a large suitcase. She moved well. Erika felt sure that whatever a camp counsellor did, Judy would be good at it. Such efficiency was a little frightening.

She asked timidly, "Could I help you?"

"Sure, you can fold the towels. Like this."

She stood watching while Erika got the first one into shape. "You're neat. You'd make a good gym teacher."

"Please?"

31

"Swimming, basketball, hockey." The long, tanned arms made descriptive gestures. "In a school, or something."

Erika smiled. "It would be nice to be a mistress," she agreed politely. She had never thought about her future before. Now for the first time it seemed likely that she would have one. Evidently it was the custom here to decide what you wanted to do while you were still in school; no one helped you make the decision.

Judy giggled. "You mean a teacher. Mistress means something different here."

"Explain me, please."

Judy sat down on the bed, elbows propped on her smooth, bare knees. "A mistress is a woman who's having a steady affair with a man. Who isn't married to him."

"I am not sure."

"Let me see, it's like this."

"I am sorry to be dumb."

"That's all right, you're not dumb. This is sort of fun," Judy told her. "Well, you know what love is? *Liebe*? What people do in bed together?"

Erika felt her face redden. "Yes, I know," she said in an almost inaudible voice.

Judy paid no attention to her embarrassment. "When two people have a love affair the woman is a mistress. Oh heck, that isn't exactly it, either."

"It is all right. I understand."

Shocked her, Judy thought. You never knew with foreigners. How did you get through to somebody who learned English in six easy lessons, or whatever it was? She said briskly, "Okay, put them in here with the handicraft stuff. Thanks a lot."

"You are then a mistress—no, a teacher in the camp?"

"Sort of. But more like a big sister. Nature study, and I'm supposed to see they don't drown or get

32

poison ivy. They're cute little squirts. Nine to eleven."

"I am sorry you have to go. Your mother and father are kind, but they are not you."

She stopped, afraid of seeming ungrateful to the Millers for all their generosity and not able, anyway, to explain what she meant. How could she say, even in her own language, that she woke up happy every morning because she would see Judy? She stood with her hands hanging at her sides, looking intently into the older girl's face.

It made Judy uneasy. The kid has a crush on me, she thought. Better put a stop to it before it gets serious. That wouldn't be so bright, especially if Peg found out. She said lightly, "It's only two weeks. I'll be back before you know it."

Then she would wait for two weeks, Erika thought. Fourteen days of feeling her way along in this strange place, learn this odd way of living, without the one thing that made it all worthwhile: Judy's casual good nature. She said, "It is so strange."

"What is?"

"Americans are wonderful. But so different."

Judy said shrewdly, "Maybe peace is always different from war. You were just a kid when the war started. If it hadn't been for Hitler your whole life would have been different."

"But not like here, I think. Not rich."

"Oh, Erika, we're not rich! My father is only an engineer and my mother does substitute teaching. They've been saving for my education since I was a baby. We're only average people."

Erika said firmly, "You are rich. You have a closet full of beautiful clothes, and your own record player. I would have been happy in the camp to have the garbage from this house."

"Yeah." Judy looked at Erika as though she had never seen her before. Erika waited for her to say,

33

as Mrs. Miller's middle-aged friends all did, "Never mind, it's all over now and you're here." As though it were indecent to look at suffering.

Instead she asked, "Why do you wear long sleeves all the time? It's too hot to wear so many clothes."

Erika's face stiffened. She had explained to Mrs. Miller, in the big glittering department store where they went to buy new clothes, that she could wear only dresses and blouses with sleeves to the wrist. Looking at her tattoo, Mrs. Miller had made no comment, only insisted that the saleslady find some long-sleeved clothes—no easy matter in this season of exposed armpits. In this house where Judy came to meals in shorts or pajamas, Erika carefully put on her new seersucker duster every time she stepped into the hall.

She unbuttoned her cuff and pulled up her sleeve. Her arms were still thin and white. The purple numerals stood out darkly in the summer light.

"Gosh. What is it?"

"My number in the camp."

Judy touched the marks with a shining fingernail. The contact made Erika shiver. "You could have it taken off," she suggested. "Plastic surgery."

Erika shook her head. "No, I keep it."

"Why?"

"I am not sure."

"It doesn't matter anyhow, nobody would think anything of it. Why don't you take off that hot old dress and get into one of my halters and get some sunshine? It's good for you. Vitamin D and all that."

Perhaps she was right. But Erika remembered the pride with which Katja had displayed her tattoo, visible sign that she had survived cold and hunger and beatings and the death of all those she loved. It was the first time she had ever heard anyone suggest that suffering was a thing to be proud of. Stein-

34

hagen had happened. She hadn't chosen it. But when someone made the same suggestion to Katja that Judy had just made to her, the Polish girl lifted her head proudly and said she intended to wear her camp number as long as she lived. "So people can never forget. So I can never forget."

Judy was going through piles of neatly folded blouses. "Here, try this for size." It was a band of material checked in red and white, no straps, with elastic woven in to keep it in place. "Take your other clothes off, silly."

She unbuttoned Erika's blouse and dropped it to the floor, although it was still quite clean. Unhooked the bra and let that fall too. Erika put up her hands to cover her almost-flat chest, feeling as though she were on fire.

"Don't be silly, You'll have to undress in front of the others when you start gym. Besides, what have you got to hide? You look like a nice little boy."

"I know it, but—"

"But nothing."

"Do girls in America show themselves like this? With nothing?"

"Some do. Not the girls I go around with, because they're different—oh, heck, skip it. You might as well get used to it."

She pulled the little strip of cloth over Erika's head and smoothed it down. It was too loose. "Have to put a safety pin in it. I'm a good four inches bigger around than you—thirty-six C, that's me." She spread her fingers over the two mounds of her high full breasts, looking embarrassed and pleased at the same time.

Before she could stop herself, before she knew what she was doing, Erika moved her hands aside. She cupped the two peaks reverently, feeling their warmth and softness through the crisp cotton of

35

Judy's blouse. For a moment the two girls stood close enough to feel each other's breathing, looking intently into each other's faces, asking and answering without words.

If she would unfasten the buttons! Erika thought, aching to uncover all that loveliness but afraid to. She remembered Katja pulling a wrinkled G.I. shirt apart to let all her richness spill out. But the need had never been this intense with Katja.

Judy moved first. She leaned forward and kissed the younger girl on the mouth. It was a hard kiss that hurt a little. Then she pushed Erika away. "Go sit in the sun for a while. It's good for you."

There was nothing to do but go.

Erika closed the bedroom door neatly behind her and walked softly through the hall and down the stairs, not wanting to talk to Mrs. Miller. She hoped that Mrs. Miller was at a club meeting, or at the beauty parlor or shopping. American women seemed to spend a great deal of time buying things and being made beautiful.

The afternoon sunshine lay brightly across the back yard, with its neat grass and colorful flower beds. Erika sat down on a plastic-covered chaise lounge, finding its striped surface less uncomfortable than she expected. The sun was hot on her neck and arms. She slipped off her loafers and wished she had a pair of sneakers; she had refused them, shocked by the extravagance, when Mrs. Miller tried to add a pair to the three pairs of shoes she had already chosen. But Judy had a dozen pairs of shoes, or more; they covered her closet floor.

Also the full, cotton skirt was hot. She needed shorts.

Her lips stung. She felt sore all over.

She sat with her head bent, in a confusion of feelings.

36

After a while her gaze fell on her left arm. The numbers glowed dark and insistent under the beating sun, larger and clearer than anything in the world—bigger than the comfortable white frame house, more real than the grass under her feet.

She was back in Steinhagen, huddled against another prisoner for warmth and reassurance, yet alone in her separate misery. The barbed wire and the injustice of man shut her in. Her body was heavy with the apathy that envelopes even the young when hunger becomes habitual. Ahead was the night, and the small, brightly lighted room where the soldiers used the younger woman prisoners for their pleasure.

She shook her head angrily to drive out the memories. I'll never let a man touch me, she thought. Never.

But it is all right. I'm in America.

She shut her eyes. Tears began to run down under the closed lids, slowly at first, as though they were heavier and more painful than mere salt water. They splashed on the red-checked cotton and left dark spots.

She couldn't remember ever crying before. When I was a baby, she thought. Some time in childhood, before I knew that tears do no good? In the camps, children learned early that no one cared whether they cried or not.

Now for the first time she felt really alone. Her father had vanished like millions of others. Her mother and little brother? Dead on a cold winter morning, their freezing blood testimony to the brutality of the conquerors. Only she was left.

Even Katja was gone, so warm and cheerful. She and Katja were a world apart, never to meet again.

She put her hands over her face and sobbed, with a deep chest-hurting intake of breath. The tears flooded over her hot and sticky face. She realized that she wasn't crying for the cold and hungry years, or the soldiers and their lust, the stolen childhood years, or even her lost family.

She was crying because Judy had kissed her, and now Judy was going to be gone fourteen long days. She was alone again.

CHAPTER SIX

"Do you feel like going to the movies?"

Carl Miller drank the last of his coffee and set down the cup. "Not unless it would break your heart to have me stay home. It's a hundred in the shade outside and sixty below indoors, with that damn air conditioning. The last time I went I had to have my sinuses drained afterward."

"Darling, your sinus trouble is psychosomatic. Dr. Conroy told you so when you had that attack last summer."

"Then my psyche and my soma are allergic to air conditioning. Why don't you and Erika go, if you don't have anything better to do?"

The English came out strong in Mrs. Miller when she was annoyed. She now said crisply, "I must say you make it sound delightful. As though only an idiot would think of wasting an evening at the cinema."

Carl lifted an eyebrow. "Well?"

"Oh, all right. Erika, do you want to go to the movies? *Kino?*"

Erika looked up from her empty dessert plate, which she had been studying through the discussion. Ordinarily she would have been delighted; she had discovered the movies with excited pleasure. Tonight she was tired and her head ached. An almost sleepless night broken by hungry thoughts of Judy, followed by a sultry day, had left her listless. She said politely, "Thank you, that will be nice."

Lucy Campbell grinned. "You sound about as enthusiastic as Carl. All right, the feature at the Tivoli starts at eight. Be sure to take a sweater. I hate to admit it, but Carl's right about the air conditioning. It's like an igloo in there."

They like each other, Erika thought wistfully, looking from one kind face to the other. They are quite old, surely more than forty, and he is a man. How can anyone want to do those disgusting things with a man? But it would be nice to belong to someone and be together every day.

She got up and began clearing the table, one of the tasks she had taken over in the week of Judy's absence from home.

"Hello, Missus Miller. Hi there." The tanned blonde in the pink shorts didn't remember Erika's name, but she wasn't embarrassed about it. She had a charming smile, consciously so. "Are you going to see the film?"

"We sure are. Where's Ken tonight? I thought you two were going steady."

"At Lake Geneva with his family. Mother's entertaining her canasta club, so I'm an orphan."

Mrs. Miller's reflexes picked up her cue. "Why don't you sit with us? Carl didn't come either."

"Love to." She gave them a bright smile. "Let me get us some popcorn. You both want some, don't you?"

Erika followed her into the lobby, pausing to admire the gilt-panelled walls, red velvet hangings and the stills of coming attractions that ornamented the Tivoli. Easels along the walls held a collection of water colors loaned by the Worthington Art League, pictures of old red barns and woodland scenes predominating. At the end of the lobby a lighted glass case held candy bars and gum, and there were shiny machines for dispensing popcorn and cold drinks.

Erika watched wide-eyed as the blonde girl dropped money in the slot, the machine released a cardboard box and a measured amount of popcorn and the mechanism turned itself off with a little click. The girl handed her the box and dropped in another dime.

Erika said, "Thank you." She couldn't remember this pleasant girl's name; these people made introductions casually or not at all, and talked to people they didn't know. It was confusing, like the way Judy's friends gathered in the kitchen. She said, "I do not remember your name. I'm sorry."

"Peg Mathes. I'm a friend of Judy's."

"I am Erika Frohmann."

"I know. I saw your picture in the paper."

Erika was embarrassed. She had hidden the clipping under her new slips and pajamas (War Orphan Guest of Carl Miller Family, Refugee Finds Welcome in Hospitable Suburb). She had meant to send it to Miss Campbell. Now she decided to wait and have a picture taken in her new clothes, with her suntan. Miss Campbell would be pleased to see her looking healthy and happy.

She followed the other two down the dark aisle, the little lights at the end of every second row glowing like little red eyes. It was shudderingly cold. She pulled on her sweater before she sat down, her shoulder almost touching Peg's.

Halfway through the feature she realized that Peg Mathes was leaning against her. At least, the length of Peg's well-tanned bare leg touched hers, and Peg's shoulder was warm and solid against her own. She stole a glance at Peg. The blonde was intent on the screen, but her eyelids flickered.

After a moment, during which Erika looked straight ahead without having the slightest idea what was happening on the screen, a small, warm hand touched hers where it hung down between the seats. Erika's fingers responded without any instruc-

41

tions from her mind. Peg's hand tightened. It was a questioning pressure, and a demanding one at the same time.

Erika sat staring blindly at the screen, across which figures without meaning now moved. She didn't know what was going to happen between her and this pretty self-assured stranger. But she knew that something was happening between them, and she wanted it to.

She was afraid, but not afraid enough to pull her hand away, although she realized that would have ended the matter. She had to know what came next. Her fingers lay smooth and unresisting in Peg's firm grasp. They stayed there through the end of the feature, the newsreel and a frightening cartoon full of animals chasing each other and beating each other up. When the lights came on again and people began to stretch and stand up, Peg dropped her hand, with a last soft pressure that she knew to be a message. They filed out into the street, Erika sharply conscious of the small, trim figure in front of her.

By this time the chill in the theater had come to seem normal. The outdoor heat met them at the door, a furnace blast. It was past ten o'clock, and the crowds had thinned, but there were still people walking around under the bright lights. The air had the sullen, heavy weight that comes before a summer thunderstorm. Mrs. Miller peeled off her cardigan. "It's inhuman. It has to break."

Peg said courteously, "Yes, we're due for rain. Do you mind if I take Erika to the Honey Bee for a coke? I'll walk her home."

"Why, thank you, dear. That's very thoughtful."

"Not at all. Would you like to come along?"

"Oh no, thanks."

Peg looked after her with bright, mocking eyes as she walked away. Anyone could tell what Mrs.

Miller was thinking: what a nice girl the Mathes youngster was and how sweet it was of her to take an interest in Erika. She was Judy's chum, in and out of the house without ringing the doorbell since they were in eighth grade together, but that didn't make her responsible for the younger girl. A kind thing to do.

She preceded Erika into a back booth at the Honey Bee. The high school crowd was beginning to thin out, boys and girls in pairs, the elite, the ones who ran things. She sat down and smoothed her hair and looked at Erika across the plastic table top. "How old are you, anyhow?"

"Sixteen. I had my birthday in May."

"I'm twenty-one, the same as Judy. We've been friends ever since we were in grade school."

Erika's face lighted at Judy's name. Peg said, smiling a little, "I guess I know more about Judy than anybody in the world. She's a real sharp girl. But she can make your life miserable if you ever let her start bossing you around."

Erika didn't answer. Peg said, "Oh, well, never mind. Can I ask you a personal question? You don't have to answer if you don't want to."

"Yes, please."

"Do you date? Go out with boys, I mean?"

Erika's eyes widened. She looked pleadingly at Peg. Peg's eyes held hers insistently. Erika said in a small voice, "No. Boys I don't know, but I do not like men, please."

"A lot of girls feel that way." Peg meant her tone to be big-sisterly and reassuring, but anxiety crept in. By her own standards this was a dangerous and foolish conversation. The kid might be shocked if she understood. Worse, she might tell Judy. She might even talk to Mrs. Miller, and that would really start something. For a moment she thought about changing the subject. Drink your coke and walk the kid home, she told herself, and don't start anything. Even if you get what you're after in this game, you lose.

Since the age of fourteen she had been building an image of herself for everyone, including her mother and father, to admire: pretty, popular, one of the crowd that counted in high school, a member of the Student Council in her first year of college. She'd suffered through dozens of dates with Big Men on Campus, letting herself be manhandled in the back seats of cars, remaining a technical virgin by the careful exercise of diplomacy. If anyone ever found out the truth about her there would be a real mess.

She was horrified to hear herself ask, "Then do you like girls? Some people do."

Erika said slowly, trying to find words for an experience kept secret and only half undertsood, "There was a girl in the Children's Camp. I don't know about this thing. Only I never want to marry a man. I hate men!"

Peg laughed harshly. "You have to play along with them just the same. Go to dances and all that jazz." She considered telling this odd little girl what the score was, then decided against it. No use taking chances. She ordered cold drinks. A waitress brought the glasses and set them down, ice cubes clinking.

Erika said, "I wish I could know. Because Katja was the only one. This is so strange for me."

Peg asked abruptly, "Are you butch?"

"Please?"

"Are you the active one? You look more like a boy than a girl."

"Oh, I would like to be a boy! Then I could have a nice girl friend who is beautiful here." She flashed a suddenly mischievous smile, putting her palms against her chest.

44

Peg laughed. "I'm kiki. I can be either, depending on who I'm with. Comes in handy sometimes." She pulled the straw out of its paper tube and stirred her drink with it. Sipping, she looked at Erika. "Do you really want to talk about this? Because you could come home and spend the night with me. It might be fun."

"But Missus Miller?"

"She won't mind. Neither will my mother. I'll call them both up and tell them."

She found some change in the pocket of her shorts and walked to the telephone booth at the back of the room. Erika sat looking after her, feeling excited and panicky at the same time. Now she was going to find out about this thing. She didn't know what was about to happen, but whatever it was, she wanted it. She had to know.

CHAPTER SEVEN

"This is my room."

Erika murmured, "Yes." There was nothing else she could say. The blonde modern furniture and soft blue curtains looked expensive, but the place was so untidy that she wondered how Peg got from the door to the bed. Dresser drawers tilted at all angles, their contents spilling out. Clothes were strewn around on chairs and even on the floor. A half-eaten apple and an empty pop bottle nudged the notebooks on the desk. The closet door stood open in a long row of dresses and a clutter of mismated shoes.

Peg didn't seem to mind. "It's a mess, isn't it? I'm supposed to take care of it myself, but there never seems to be any time. Every once in a while Mom lowers the boom on me, and I shovel out."

Erika said, "Yes," again. Noticing that although Peg, like Judy, was an only child, the room had identical twin beds with soft blue covers. One was neatly made up under heaps of records and books, the other a tumble of squashed pillow and dragging sheets. Peg caught the look. "You can have the made one. It's too hot to need anything but bottom sheets anyhow."

It was after eleven. Erika was wet with sweat, her head ached, but she was far from sleepy. She wanted to learn everything about this girl.

Peg yawned widely. "Gosh, it's hot in here. Dad's going to put in an air conditioner next year, now wartime restrictions are off, but we'll all be dead with the heat by that time." She bent to untie her sneakers. Erika noticed that her toenails were painted with the same color as her fingernails, and her lipstick matched both.

"Want a shower? There's clean towels on the shelf, and different kinds of soap in the cabinet if you don't like what's opened. I'll find you a pair of pajamas. Unless you'd rather sleep raw—I always do, it's more comfortable."

Erika reddened. "I would like the pajamas, please."

"Sure. Gosh, you're polite! Are all Europeans as polite as you?"

"I don't know. Besides, I am not so polite. Often I cannot understand what people are saying."

"You do all right." Peg was tumbling garments out of dresser drawers, dropping them on the floor. She came up with a pair of baby doll pajamas in thin flowered cotton. "These are too big, but it's more comfortable that way."

Erika carried them to the bathroom, which was tidy. The contrast with Peg's room was startling. She pulled off her clothes and got into the shower. The cool water felt good. She stood holding a big bar of soap, lost in her own physical sensations.

She had never thought much about her body. In the prison camp, cold and hunger were its daily experience, pain and humiliation frequent and unavoidable. Now her whole body sparkled with excitement. She ran her hands over her bosom, and the little pink buds hardened and rose to her touch. At the very core of her being, a strange feeling gathered and grew insistent. She wanted something—she didn't know what it was, but she wanted it intensely.

She seized a washcloth and began soaping herself, turning the water on full force to take her mind off the way she felt. She was frightened by the intensity of her own desire.

The pajamas were loose on her, but short and almost transparent. She looked at her reflection in the

47

long mirror on the bathroom door and was embarrassed. At the same time she couldn't help feeling pleased because she had a good body, still thin, but beginning to fill out. Her skin was white and smooth, and she moved well. Her eyes looked back at her, wide and excited.

She went back to Peg's room, resisting a nervous impulse to put her hands protectively in front of her.

Peg had shucked off her shorts and tee shirt, and sat on the unmade bed clothed only in two narrow strips of fabric. She was sorting records and fitting them into their paper jackets as though it were the most important job in the world. She smiled at Erika. "Feel better? I'll go and get myself cooled off." She stood up and stretched, every line of her well-developed young body sharp in the overhead light.

Erika stood still, the strange urgent feeling growing stronger, wondering what was happening to her. It was a relief when Peg walked out of the room. Because the feeling was tied in with Peg, whom she had never seen until tonight. It was a crazy need to be close to Peg, so close they were like one person.

Peg smiled, pulling off her panty and bra and stepping into the shower. She had a thing or two to settle with Judy Miller. There was the matter of the ballet dancer Judy had been cruising last winter—with what results Peg hadn't been able to find out, but Judy had certainly gone around looking smug for a while. And on two different occasions when they were spending the night together, Judy had teased and tempted her beyond the point of no resistance, and then turned over and pretended to go to sleep. How bitchy could a girl get?

Besides—she caught her breath as the cold water hit—she liked Erika Frohmann. She was kind of a pathetic little kid, but there was something about her. And she had a hungry look that was all too familiar to Peg. You didn't have to be a refugee or an orphan to look like that. She'd felt that way herself before Judy brought her out—and since, sometimes.

Shall I call her to come and scrub my back or something? No, she decided. This one will scare easy. Play it cool. One wrong move and she's likely to run away or faint or something. Or tell.

She hadn't bothered to provide pajamas for herself. She shrugged. Plenty of people slept bare. She hung up the damp towels, since her mother did enforce order in the family bathroom, and tiptoed back to her bedroom. And Erika.

Erika was sitting on the guest bed, doing nothing. Her eyes widened when she saw Peg. The color crept up her neck and spread over her face, but she didn't look away. Peg said carelessly, "I hate to wear anything in hot weather. Do you mind?" She bent to pick up the last of the records, placing them carefully on the floor. Her swinging breasts, soft yet firm, almost touched Erika's arm. Erika looked at them, fascinated.

Peg said casually, "Better get to bed. It's been a long hot day. I sure hope the heat wave breaks pretty soon."

"Yes, so do I."

Erika stood aside as her hostess turned down the top sheet, then the spread. She got a whiff of Peg's spicy dusting powder, and it made her feel a little dizzy. Peg said, "It's too hot for anything. There you are—yell if you want anything."

She swept the debris on her own bed to the floor, and turned off the ceiling light. In the pale glimmer from the open window Erika saw her stretch out on the other bed, the pale curving length of her uncovered to the night air.

What I want cannot be yelled for, Erika thought.

With increasing urgency she wanted to touch that beautiful young body, to hold it close against her, to cover it from head to toe with passionate kisses. And more. She didn't know what "more" was, the brief stolen moments with Katja hadn't taught her what lay beyond their caresses, but she felt there must be some way to satisfy the hunger that consumed her.

She touched herself inquiringly, then remembered that if she could see Peg in the semi-darkness, Peg could also see her. She lay back with her arms under her head.

It was very hot. Already the borrowed pajamas felt damp and wrinkled, the lower sheet rumpled. She pulled up her knees to ease the tension, but it didn't help. She was wide-awake and alert in every muscle.

Thunder muttered and grumbled on the far horizon. Then the whole sky lightened. A moment later came the sharp crack of the thunder. Erika screamed. The sound split the air in the room before she knew it was going to happen. She cowered in the narrow bed, ashamed of her terror but frightened just the same.

Peg was beside her, bending over her. She said softly, "What's the matter?"

"I am sorry. It sounds like shooting."

"You poor baby." Peg's hand touched her as the lightning crashed again, a wide searing light that showed every detail of her naked body. She gathered Erika in and held her close, with the younger girl's head cradled against her bosom. For a moment they were motionless and silent.

Then Peg said, "There, you're all right now." She lay down, pulling Erika down beside her. Crowded together on the single bed, Erika became aware of the hard breast bud pressing into her cheek. She turned her head so that her mouth touched it inquiringly, then closed around it.

"That's right. That's the way."

"Peg."

"What is it, honey?"

"I don't know what's the matter with me, I feel so strange."

"I'll show you."

It was beginning to rain. A cool wind blew the curtains inward, and the first drops splashed on the porch floor under the bedroom window. The drops came faster and harder. Peg said absently, "It's raining in. The hell with it."

Her hand moved over Erika's shoulders, across her back, then around to investigate the adolescent curves of her bosom. "Do you like it when I do this?"

"I like better to touch you."

"Why not?" Peg shifted so that one arm lay across Erika's hips. "How's that?"

This was pleasure and excitement such as Erika had never known before, nor even imagined. She gave herself to it. Outside, the rain settled to a steady downpour.

The feeling in her was stronger now. She had to satisfy it, and she didn't know how. She said hesitantly, stammering in an agony of desire, "I—I don't know what is the matter. I have this feeling."

"Show me."

She couldn't answer. Peg's hand moved, found what she was seeking, stopped. "Here?"

"Yes."

Peg giggled. Erika raised her head and gave her a hurt and astonished look. Peg said, "That's easy." She detached herself very gently from Erika's arm and changed her position on the bed. Erika lay on her back waiting for she didn't know what, feeling the pressure of Peg's lips against her skin. The lips moved lower and became insistent. Erika gasped.

"You do it for me too. Like this."

Now she was pulled into a whirlpool of feeling, a wild excitement that rose in the center of her body and flowed into every part of her. A series of electric shocks mounted in voltage so that she had to cry out, she couldn't help it. The feeling was all that mattered. She no longer existed, or the bed, or the room, or even Peg except as seeking lips and probing tongue and caressing hands. Only the feeling was real.

She heard herself making strange sounds in her throat as it became unbearable. Then the wave broke. The fountain of desire became a flood that swept her away. Wave after wave washed over her.

Then she was lying on a narrow bed with Peg's hand gently patting her, as hot and swollen flesh subsided and feeling diminished. Peg's head lay damp and heavy against her hip. She relaxed, filled with a wonderful peace and calm. A cool wind blew through the room and over their sweat-drenched bodies.

Outside, the rain strummed steadily against the waiting ground, which lay like a woman thirsty and open for love.

CHAPTER EIGHT

AUGUST SECOND. Sunshine lay across the floor in long broken strips; under the drawn shades little gold specks danced in the morning light. Erika lay on her back with her eyes half shut, sorting out the day.

Judy! she thought, bouncing out of bed and feeling her grin grow from ear to ear. The fourteen days that had stretched ahead so endlessly were over and Judy would be home this afternoon. She shivered with pleasure.

Lucy Miller called from the foot of the stairs, "Erika, are you awake?"

"That's all right, Missus Miller." Peg's voice. "I'll go up."

The soft patter of sneakers crossed the front hall and was lost on the stair carpet. Erika stood beside the bed, wide-eyed and breathing hard, not sure she wanted to see Peg. She hadn't heard her voice since the morning after the storm. But she had done a good deal of thinking.

And feeling, too. A mixture of physical pleasure that drove her to experiment when she was alone, in an attempt to produce it for herself; renewed hunger for the strange caresses Peg had taught her; a secret dread of their next meeting. I'll be calm, she promised herself. I'll wait for her to make the first move. But Peg had neither dropped in nor called.

There was a sharp tap on the bedroom door. Peg pushed it open and walked in without waiting for an invitation. "Hi there. Did I get you out of bed?"

"No, I was awake." The pajamas Mrs. Miller had bought for her were more concealing than the pair

Peg had first lent her and then pulled off, but Erika felt embarrassed even though a furtive glance at the mirror assured her she was decently covered. She crossed her arms over her chest and stood looking at the older girl, a little frightened and not knowing what to say.

Peg looked calm. Her eyes were clear blue in the even tan of her face, her lips were a smooth orange-red, and against the well-pressed shorts and shirt her arms were almost copper. She could have posed for a magazine advertisement, one of a group of happy teenagers beside a pool, holding a bottle of some carbonated drink. Beside her, Erika felt tousled and awkward. She turned around to look for her robe, but it was hanging in the closet.

Peg smiled. "Are you mad at me?"

"No, not at all."

"You didn't call or anything."

"I didn't know—I was not sure you wanted me to. I'm sorry."

Peg sighed. "Boy or butch, no matter who you're going with it's the same old story—sit around and wait for the phone to ring. It's too much." She looked sharply at Erika's puzzled face, and laughed. "It's all right. Don't look like that."

Erika said bashfully, "I wanted to call you." It sounded like an excuse, and a flimsy one at that. How was she to explain that talking on the telephone made her nervous, made her forget her still-hesitant English?

Besides, she thought unhappily, she wouldn't have known what to say. There are some things you can't discuss on the telephone.

Peg moved closer. "Did you tell anybody about the other night?"

"No." How could she have told anyone, when she was afraid even to think about it in the daytime, in case someone might read the guilt and longing on her face? At night, alone in the dark, she could take the incredible memory of those hours out of her mind and live it again—but would she tell anyone, ever?

"Don't ever." Peg's voice dropped. There was a threatening note in it. "Because they'll crucify you if they even suspect you're gay. Straight people are all alike."

"But why?" Curiosity got the better of fear. "I can see that most women like men. They marry and have babies. But the other, for two people only—why should anyone care?"

Peg's smile was chilly. "It sounds reasonable, but it doesn't work out that way. They act like we were criminals or outcasts. Two girls got kicked out of the freshman class last year because of gossip. Just rumors, you know, they couldn't prove anything, but the faculty found excuses to let them go."

"Is it against the law then, this love?"

"Oh, law! No more than a lot of things straight people do. In some states it's even against the law for husbands and wives to try any variations when they make love. No," Peg said seriously, forgetting to be on guard, "straight men can rape and murder little girls, they can spread disease all over the place and get young girls pregnant, but that's all right. That's normal," Peg said bitterly. She sounded as though all this had been simmering in her mind for a long time.

"It's wrong, then?"

"Do you think so?"

She didn't know what she thought. For almost a week she had been in a tumult of feeling, passionate and frightened, but the question of right and wrong hadn't entered into it. She would have to think about it from that angle. But, she thought, if it doesn't hurt anybody how can it be wrong?

"Come on, get your clothes on. Missus Miller's making breakfast for you."

Erika understood that the discussion of lesbian love was over so far as Peg was concerned. And nothing more was going to happen between them—she knew that without being told, although she didn't know why. Peg's only worry was that she might tell.

She wondered about Katja. Did she know there were other people like this in the world? Or had she stumbled by instinct upon this way of loving that less needy people found so evil, just because she too had been turned against men by their violence and selfishness? All that warmth and kindness reaching out to the warmth in another human being—was it that way for everyone, for straight people too, and if so, did they ever find what they were looking for?

She didn't see why it should matter except to the two who were involved.

She didn't want to dress in front of Peg now that there was nothing between them, not even a possibility of real friendship. She picked out some clean clothes and took them into the bathroom, leaving Peg to look moodily out of the bedroom window.

I need someone to love, Erika decided, getting into the shorts and shirt that were now her daytime uniform and tying the laces of her white sneakers. Everybody needs love. Even a little bit of affection would be better than nothing at all. People will hang on to a halfway romance that doesn't really mean much to either of them, if it's the best they have.

She remembered friendships begun in the camp, for no reason that anybody could see; when one woman died of cold or hunger or dysentery, the other soon lost her grip on life. Yet there was no sex in that, nobody had energy enough to make love even if the necessary privacy had been available. What was it, then? Did everyone feel incomplete alone?

56

She trailed silently down the stairs after Peg and into the sunny kitchen where Mrs. Miller was setting two places at the snack counter. Erika still wasn't used to seeing people eat in the kitchen. The girls sat side by side drinking tomato juice and eating scrambled eggs while Mrs. Miller had her second cup of coffee and talked about shopping lists. Peg's answers were bright and automatic; Erika was silent.

They looked like pictures in a glossy magazine, she thought, not for the first time. Two young girls and an attractive mother in a colorful modern kitchen. Except for the purple tattoo on her arm, reminding her that she didn't really belong in all this plenty and sunshine, in this strange country.

But the depression lifted after Peg went home. By four o'clock, when the Miller car drew up in front of the bus station, she didn't mind Peg's already being there. She waited tensely for Judy to materialize among all these shouting children and fussing parents. When she finally swung down from the chartered bus, looking exactly as she had two weeks before, it was an anticlimax. It's only Judy, Erika thought, mildly surprised. Why was I so upset?

For a moment her daydreams of Judy seemed pale and trivial alongside the secret remembered excitement of Peg's knowing hands and searching mouth.

She made her greeting casual. After all, only two weeks. Only summer camp. Judy had not been in any danger. The three girls were sitting in the back seat of the Miller car before she fully realized that Peg was coming with them. Why, on this first day?

Why should Peg grab Judy's suitcase and duffle bag and carry them up the front stairs to Judy's room, as though they were her own luggage? Why should she go into the bedroom with Judy and shut the door, in this house where doors stood open most of the time? Erika, standing at the foot of the stairs

57

with the overflow from Judy's possessions, looked blankly at Mrs. Miller. Judy's mother said gently, "The girls are chums, you know. They'll have a lot to talk about. Judy will want to visit with you later."

She realized, with a shock, that she wasn't wanted. She put down the handicraft clutter, the notebooks and braided lanyards very carefully, as though they might break, and walked through the house and into the back yard. On tiptoe, as though noise might bother someone. Who?

She sat down on the aluminum and plastic chaise and wrapped her arms around her pulled-up knees. The tattooed numbers stood out against her white skin.

She felt like crying, and she didn't know why.

There was a small sound from the upstairs window. She looked up, willing to be distracted from her sadness.

Judy was pulling down the windowshade. She was laughing, and as she turned Erika saw that she was naked from the waist up. Her beautiful breasts stood out boldly. Someone put an arm around her and pulled her backward. The tan cloth shade came down and hid her from sight.

Suddenly Erika knew what was happening. She knew why Peg had been so final about putting their brief affair in the past tense and why she had chosen this day for her visit, to assure herself of Erika's silence.

Her face set coldly. She got up from the chaise and walked along the side of the garage and out into the alley where the garbage cans stood. A neighbor boy, emptying a wastebasket, gave her a friendly hello. She didn't see or hear him.

She walked fast, not caring where she went so long as it was away from that house, where the only two people who mattered to her were in bed together.

CHAPTER NINE

SHE NEEDED darkness and silence. A place to hide. But the wide, bright downtown streets of Worthington lay exposed to the heat of the Midwestern afternoon, and in the smooth faces of the shopping women there was no knowledge of trouble. She stood in the middle of the sidewalk not knowing where to go or what to do, and people walked around her.

A glitter caught her eye. Across the street the marquee of a movie house twinkled in competition with the sunshine. Blown-up stills pictured a busty blonde wih an idiotic smile, a dissipated-looking man in the garb of a gentleman gambler of the Nineties and a noble young man in a ten-gallon hat. Erika's mind jumped back to her last evening at the movies, sandwiched between Mrs. Miller and Peg. It wouldn't be quiet with the sound-track blasting, but it would be dark and no one would know her.

She felt in the pocket of her shorts, her lips moving as she counted her change—she still had trouble with nickels and quarters. The traffic light was green. She crossed the street absent-mindedly and bought a ticket from the bored girl at the window.

The inside of the building was dark and teeth-chatteringly cold. She sat near the front, wishing she had a coat. After a few minutes the darkness thinned and lightened, and people sprang into being around her—dark shapes all facing the screen, moving now and then. She closed her eyes to make them disappear, just as the florid opening music introduced the feature film.

She had expected to feel sad, since Peg had withdrawn her desire and Judy her casual good nature. The one was not love, nor the other friendship, but they were all she'd had and now she had nothing. But alone in the dark, with time to explore her feelings, she found she was without any. She felt empty and blank. It was like the worst days in the camp, when thought and emotion were suspended and survival was just a matter of time.

There were little sounds around her, whispers, and feet scuffling, and the dry rattle of popcorn in cardboard boxes. If she opened her eyes there would be figures moving across the screen. She didn't want to be bothered. She wanted to understand what was happening to her.

She wanted to cry, but she had forgotten how.

She tried to think about Peg, then about Judy, but neither girl seemed real to her. They were like people she had heard about a long time ago.

Someone sat down beside her. She felt rather than saw the man as he pushed down the folding seat and settled his weight into it. He was close enough for her to be aware of his bulk and body heat and a definite male odor. She thought of changing her seat, but there was only one empty place between her and a pair of whispering and kissing high-schoolers and she didn't want to sit next to them. She shut her eyes and tried to recapture her aloneness.

But the sound track kept breaking in and the newcomer's heavy breathing was an added irritant. All right then—she would move to the back row. She opened her eyes and, turning her head, saw that the man—boy, really—in the end seat was looking at her. And that his leg, in the tight-fitting white of a sailor's summer uniform, was stretched across the end of the row to bar her exit.

He smiled, not unpleasantly. He was not more than twenty, with nice white teeth and a mop of light curls under the little pushed-back cap. She looked away.

He laid his hand on her knee, a big, warm, heavy male hand. She tried to move away, but the stiff arms of the seat held her. The hand moved too, resting for a moment on her knee and then inching higher, warm on the chilled flesh of her inner thigh.

She started to rise. The hand pressed her down. The boy said in a loud whisper, "Don't be mad at me, I'm not going to do anything." He smiled again, like a child who has learned to get his own way by being winsome.

I can scream, Erika thought. If I screamed, surely someone would come to help me. She visualized it: the turning heads, the babble of voices, the arrival of an usher—maybe a policeman?—and the turning on of the house lights.

She opened her mouth, but no sound came out.

The sailor said, "You want to have some fun? C'mon, let's not watch this. Let's go for a walk or something."

"Go away."

"Oh baby, don't be like that. You're beautiful. You're the most beautiful girl I've seen since I hit this square town. How about it?"

Erika looked stonily at the screen. The blonde was kissing the gambler, while a full orchestra played somewhere—in the magnolia trees, probably.

The hand crept a little higher. His other arm draped itself carelessly around her shoulders. After a moment the fingers moved around to cup a breast. She twitched away, but he followed her.

"Come on, don't be scared. Let's go someplace and have a beer or something. I won't hurt you. What could I do right out in broad daylight?"

The couple on the screen were now clenched in an impassioned embrace, the girl's hands clutching

61

her lover's fully-clothed back, although both faces were blank of expression.

The boy said, wheedling, "Aw, come on. What have you got to do that's so important?"

It was a slap in the face. She turned and looked at him, wide-eyed.

Because she had nothing to do and no place to go. In the Miller house, Judy and Peg were making love in a darkened bedroom and Mrs. Miller was going innocently about her housework, pleased to have her daughter home again, accepting the friendship at its face value. Breathe the air in that house while Peg was there? It was impossible.

She couldn't stay here with people looking at her, while a man's hand fondled her leg and another tried to get down inside her shirt. Already the adolescents in the next seats had stopped giggling and were watching her curiously. And she was too tired to walk up and down the hot streets among all these people who had places to go and things to do, jobs and homes and people who belonged to them, while she belonged nowhere and had no one.

Besides, she realized in sudden fright, this idiot might follow her, talking in that soft, coaxing, fake-tender voice. The embarrassment would be too much.

Her indecision seemed to give him courage. After all, he was very young. He cleared his throat and said again, "How about it? Come on, we'll have something to eat and talk things over. I got a nice cool hotel room with air conditioning."

Erika said shortly, "I don't want anything to eat."

"You come up to the room a while, then?"

"Yes."

Because it didn't matter. Nothing mattered. She was nobody.

She got up and followed him out of the theater. It seemed to her that their footsteps made a thunderous noise on the carpeted aisle, although no one looked up.

Out on the sidewalk, under the merciless sun, he looked her over. She met his eyes without caring, seeing in his face all the good-natured young servicemen she had seen since she came to America, a healthy and not very bright boy out to celebrate his leave with drink, sex, and late sleeping.

If he was disappointed in her, he didn't show it. He asked, "How old are you? I can't get served in a bar because I haven't got an ID. I'll be twenty-one in a couple months, though."

"I'm eighteen." An automatic lie, knowing that he wouldn't feel so guilty afterwards if he thought she was an adult.

He took her hand in his, like a child. "You real sure you don't want something to eat? Like a hamburger, maybe?"

"Nothing."

"Come on, then. What are we waiting for?"

He put a hand through her arm, hugging up against her. She walked beside him, paying no more attention to the insinuating white-sleeved arm than if it had been a block of wood.

"What's your name, hon?"

With sudden malice: "Peg."

"Gee, that's a pretty name. I'm Bob Anderson. From Minnesota—the woods are full of Andersons up there."

She supposed she ought to say something, to keep a wall of talk between them, but she didn't know what. She looked ahead, feeling her face cold and stony.

He said with young boastfulness, "I got a bottle of vodka in my hotel room. You can get a bottle in Chicago without an ID, plenty of places, if you know where to look."

She didn't answer.

He pressed her arm tighter against his side, giving her a meaningful look. "You're cute. Wait till we get up to the room and you have a good drink. That'll loosen you up."

"Yes."

"You're not much of a talker, are you? Cat got your tongue?"

"I never talk much."

"Actions speak louder than words, that's what they say. I bet you're a hot number in the sack."

The sidewalk was cracked. She stumbled, seized his arm, and righted herself. The sickness was growing in her; she could taste it in the back of her mouth, bitter and metallic, as she had on those nights in the Herr Kapitan's office.

He gave her a look full of meaning. "Here we are! Don't say anything, just follow me. Isn't anybody going to ask a serviceman in uniform any questions."

She hadn't known what to expect: a squalid dive full of criminal types or a Hollywood palace of sin. She followed Bob Anderson across the fairly clean, fairly well-furnished lobby under the incurious eyes of a desk clerk to whom sailors with dames were plainly a nickel a dozen.

This one looks like jail bait, he thought. Tramps! But he didn't really care. Boys were something else again—if a boy came in here with a serviceman, you could shake them down yourself or call the vice squad and hope for a payoff. But hell, where girls are concerned everybody expects a serviceman to get all he can. That's what leaves are for.

The self-service elevator made her feel faint and panicky, as always. It didn't matter. The cage stopped and the door slid open. She followed him down a hall of shut doors, with radio music coming from behind some of them, and waited while he found the key in his blouse pocket and unlocked a door that looked like all the rest.

I could still leave, she reminded herself. I could run away. But she followed him into the room, which was cool and had a double bed neatly made up and, in one corner, a half-unpacked seabag.

The boy put his arms around her and kissed her. His body was big and muscular and he held her tightly. He smelled like cigarettes and shaving lotion and sweat and something else—an odor she recognized as the male in heat. It made her feel even sicker.

His mouth was hot and thick on hers, his tongue pushed her lips open, pressed between her clenched teeth and then seemed to fill and overflow her mouth, choking her. She wanted to beg him to stop, but no words could get past that barrier.

She stood still and unmoving until he was satisfied.

After a while he stepped back, giving her a smile bright with fatuous good will. "You want a drink now, baby? Sit down on the bed and cool off while I fix us a nice drink. Can you take vodka with just water or shall I send down for some cubes?"

"It doesn't matter."

She thought it was probably the first liquor he had ever bought. Probably he had paid more than it was worth because he wasn't old enough to buy it legally.

He brought her a plastic tumbler from the bathroom, with about an inch of lukewarm water in it, and carefully poured out the liquor. He looked so proud and pleased that for a moment she almost liked him.

They are so young, she thought. Like children. They don't know the way things really are. And so many of them never grow up.

He put the glass in her hand. The contents were faintly warm and colorless, like water. She held it loosely, trying to get enough courage for the first taste.

He pulled her down beside him on the edge of the bed. The springs creaked under their combined weight. He said, "Drink up, baby. It'll make you feel great. I'm going to love you like you never been loved before."

CHAPTER TEN

EVERYTHING WAS getting blurry and far away. Her body didn't belong to her any more. She touched her bare knee, inquiringly, and both hand and knee acknowledged the touch, but when she stood up and walked unsteadily into the bathroom, her body seemed to be floating along while she stood off at one side and looked at it. Her own face was unfamiliar and big-eyed in the bathroom mirror.

She drifted back into the bedroom and saw that Bob Anderson had poured himself another drink—his third, fourth, she had lost count. His face looked vague. He grinned at her. "Feel better?"

"I am all right."

Thinking, why in hell doesn't he do it and get it over with? All these games he plays.

As if he had read her mind, he put his glass down on the floor and walked over to where she stood. There was a silence broken only by the sound of his breathing while he gave her another of the suffocating tongue kisses. She was relieved when he stopped and, instead, began running exploring hands over her body.

She stood still while he felt the curves of her breasts and hips, put a hand down the neck of her shirt and the shoulder seam ripped, but he ignored it and went on with his search. Finally he got the shirt off by jerking it roughly over her head and then, with quite a bit of fumbling, undid the little hook at the back of her bra.

"Oh baby, you're pretty. Maybe there ain't much

there but it's all you, no kidding. Let me look at those—"

He was busy, then, with fingers and eventually lips. She remembered how good it had been when Peg did the same thing, and shuddered. Bob Anderson mistook her tremor for rising desire. His hand went up inside her skirt and found what he wanted.

There was quite a lot of this before he pulled off the wrinkled white shorts, the cotton panty, and the sneakers. She looked down and saw her naked body emerge in the late afternoon sunlight. It was all familiar, yet it was like looking at someone else.

She hadn't seen him take off his own clothes, yet there he was, his big, meaty, muscular body free from the tight summer whites. She decided wisely that she must be a little bit drunk herself. It was the first time she had ever seen a completely naked man, and for a moment she was curious. From the detached place in which she seemed to be operating, she gave him a long inquisitive look. Ugly, she thought.

Fear swept through her. Let me out of here! It was a silent scream that no one heard, certainly not the boy. She stepped back to evade his groping hands.

The edge of the bed caught her behind the knees. She wavered. He caught her and pulled her down beside him on the hotel bedspread. His body pressed against her, heavy and hard and wet with sweat. She tried to pull away. He grabbed her with both hands and then the entire weight of him was pinning her to the bed. Then he took her, without a preliminary caress or word. It was like being split in two. The wind was knocked out of her; she tried to catch her breath and couldn't. His mouth came down on hers, shutting off speech.

When she was a very small girl, walking with her father through the summer countryside, she had seen a workman hammering railroad spikes. The great iron sledge came down on the metal spike, and the wooden crossbar groaned like a woman in pain as the clang of metal splintered the soft summer air. Again and again and again. The little girl stood terrified with her hands over her ears, waiting for that ruthless hammering to stop.

Now the hammer blows were inside her body, and the echo reverberated through her. Again, again, and again.

No more, she begged without words. I can't, I can't! But all that came out of her mouth was a muffled sob, and he paid no attention.

Until finally he lifted his head to mutter something she couldn't understand, and the hammering speeded up. Then he groaned deeply and his body jerked and shuddered and was still.

He rolled off. Air rushed into her cramped lungs. She had forgotten how sweet it was to breathe freely. She was terribly tired. Eyes half shut, she decided she would never feel rested again.

The boy rolled over heavily and reached out to pat her shoulder. "You want a drink, kid? I'm going to fix me one." He grinned proudly, adding something she didn't understand but from the way he said it she knew the words were dirty. "Maybe we'll have a second helping later on, huh?"

Erika sat up. The room swung dizzily around. She focussed her eyes on the opposite wall until it righted itself, a trick she had learned in the hungriest days. Bob Anderson got out of bed and stood with his back to her, pouring the last of the vodka into the plastic tumbler. His buttocks jiggled as he moved.

She picked her shorts off the floor and fumbled to turn them right-side out.

"Hey, what you doing? You going bashful on me or something?" With a pleased grin. "You don't have to put your clothes on to go to the john, if that's what's on your mind."

She stepped into the shorts, which stuck to her clammy skin, and managed to fasten the waistband button. The shirt was easier. There was a familiar moment of fright as she pulled it over her head. What if he grabbed her while her eyes were covered? Then her face emerged and she got her arms into the sleeves and walked to the door.

"Hey, where do you think you're going? Come back here!"

She stumbled on something. A white canvas oxford, scuffed and dirty now. From long habit (shoes were precious, when a prisoner died you took off his shoes before you turned the body over to the guards) she bent quickly and scooped up the sneaker, then its mate. And reached for the doorknob with her free hand.

The door was locked. The boy was on his feet staring at her, his face more puzzled than angry. He wasn't a bright boy, and sex and vodka and male egotism all blended together in him to prevent his understanding, right away, that things were not all right. He took a step in her direction, but she found the lock and shifted the button. The door swung open on an empty electric-lighted hallway.

Bob Anderson realized that he was naked, and hesitated.

Erika rushed down the hall. Beside the elevator grille a dimly-lighted flight of stairs led down. She ran down, stumbling, righting herself, sobbing under her breath, cursing in German—and clutching the shoes.

It was four or five flights to the ground floor, she didn't know exactly how many. At one landing a man with a briefcase looked after her with his mouth in an

O of astonishment. Thinks I'm a thief, she realized with a nervous giggle. It didn't matter. All that mattered was to get away from the naked sailor upstairs before he could start the hammering again.

At the end of the last flight she recognized the lobby, the framed oil painting she had noticed when she first came in and the desk clerk looking bored. She leaned against the newel post and pulled on the sneakers, and then walked quickly across the lobby and out into the street without looking around to see who had observed her or what, if anything, the faces registered.

It was about eight o'clock, still daylight, but the air was beginning to soften. A slight breeze ruffled her hair and felt good against her wet skin. She walked briskly around the corner, looked back to make sure no one was following her, and stood for a moment against the wall of a hamburger place, getting her breath and her bearings.

She had no money. But the shopping district of the rich little suburb was familiar to her now from the many buying trips she had made with Mrs. Miller. She was perhaps ten or twelve blocks from home, within easy walking distance.

For the first time since her arrival in the United States she realized that the Miller house was the only home she had. Some day, perhaps, she would find a place where she really belonged. It was too far in the future to think about. For now she was completely dependent upon the kindness of these good-hearted strangers.

She was as much a prisoner as she had been at Steinhagen. A well-fed prisoner with plenty to eat, a room of her own and a shower at the end of her forced march.

She began to walk. Her legs and back ached, and

on her arms bruises were darkening to match her serial number. She saw the marks and felt the pain, but neither seemed important.

Even with the soldiers it had never hurt so much.

I will never let a man touch me again, she resolved. Never. Not even if they kill me for resisting.

CHAPTER ELEVEN

IT WAS growing dark by the time she got in, and as luck would have it, Carl and Lucy Miller were sitting on the front porch with the overhead light off, quietly enjoying an hour together as they liked to do. Lucy asked anxiously, "What in the world happened to you? We finally went ahead and ate but then we started to get worried. I was about ready to call the police."

Erika stood on the bottom step with a hand over her torn shirt, keeping her face in the shadow. "I am so sorry. I went to a movie. It was a very long one."

"Well, you're here all right now. Can you fix yourself some supper, or shall I come in and heat something up for you?"

She saw that Mrs. Miller was tired. Too, she enjoyed sitting in the semi-dark with her husband, talking a little and then falling into a relaxed silence. Their leisure didn't often coincide; she was busy with housework and community enterprises and, during the school year, substitute teaching. Erika said, "Oh, no, I make something, but first I will have a shower, please."

"Sure has been a hot day," Carl Miller agreed.

She walked past them quickly, before they could notice the torn shirt and dirty shorts and smell the sweat and fear and the man's odor on her. The screen door closed quietly behind her.

Lucy Miller said, "Imagine, a teenager who doesn't slam doors. Only she sounded—you suppose something's wrong?"

"Homesick, most likely."

"For a Nazi prison camp? You're out of your mind."

73

Carl Miller was a perceptive man. "Sometimes a person's homesick and doesn't know what for."

The front steps were familiar to Erika's feet; the railing slid comfortably under her hand. In these weeks her body, at least, had come to be at home in this house. The bathroom doorknob turned easily under her fingers. She pushed the door open, thinking only of soap and hot water.

Judy bent over the basin, naked, drying her hair. She heard the door open, and turned. Erika stood in the doorway, sweaty, bruised, puffy-lipped, sagging against the jamb; clothes torn and soiled. Judy said, "Well. Steam roller run over you?"

Erika pressed her lips tightly together. The truth was impossible and she was too tired to think of a good lie. She shook her head mutely. The motion made her feel sick.

Judy's arms shot out. She grabbed Erika by the shoulders and shook her, hard. "Damn it, don't you shake your head at me. What happened to you?"

The truth flew out in spite of her intentions. "I went with a sailor."

"You mean he raped you?"

"No. I went with him."

"That was a damn stupid thing to do. You might have been murdered or something."

"I didn't care."

"But why?" Judy looked at her. "I don't get it."

Erika realized that everything was lost anyway. She said simply, "Because you were with Peg. Up here."

Judy looked stunned. "Are you off your rocker over Peg, or what?"

"No. You."

As soon as she heard the two syllables echoing on the steamy air she wished she had died in that horrible hotel room. Or at Steinhagen, she thought miserably.

Judy said, "Oh. I see." She wrapped the towel around her dripping head and tucked the ends in to make a turban. Erika stood with her head down, waiting for the blow, wondering whether it would be verbal or physical. In either case she was too tired to dodge.

Judy said in her mother's sensible voice, "Run yourself a good hot bath, as hot as you can stand it, and get in."

She stayed in the room, sitting on the laundry hamper, while Erika scrubbed and dried herself. "Feel better?"

"I could sleep a long time."

Judy followed her into her neat bedroom, shook out a pair of clean pajamas and held them while she got into them. Then she sat down on the edge of the bed, beside Erika's still tense body. Under the pink towel her face was determined.

"Now what's all this about? How did Peg get into it?"

Erika closed her eyes. Behind the lids, red circles wheeled slowly. "I stayed at her house one time. She did something," she said slowly. She didn't want to talk about Peg; she wanted to go to sleep and never wake up. But Judy was waiting.

She tried to explain, not knowing the words for much of what she had to tell. It was plain from Judy's expression that she was angry, but Erika wasn't sure at whom. Finally she said, "That bitch. Just because she was angry at me."

Erika put a hand to her mouth. "I was not supposed to tell."

"That's all right. She meant not to tell straight people, like Mother and Dad. They'd never understand." Judy sighed. "I don't think parents ever understand their children, anyhow."

75

Erika's eyes asked the question she was afraid to put into words. Judy said crossly, "Don't be stupid." But she sounded worried, as though saying it out loud gave the fact a reality it didn't have before.

"Do you love her?"

"Oh, love!" Judy thought it over. "Well, yes, she's good in bed. And she's kiki—I mean she'll do either part, active or passive or both at once, though I don't know what's so damn passive about it if you respond at all. It's fun to change off once in a while." She shifted on the bed, moving closer to Erika. "Most people think a gay girl has to be either femme or butch all the time. Some are, some aren't. I can be either. In fact, I'm probably bi—I'll probably end up married to some nice square boy with a college degree and an office job and have three or four kids and a house in the suburbs. With a barbecue pit."

Erika didn't understand all of that, but enough came through to open her drooping eyelids. So the two worlds mixed, and some people went back and forth between them, like commuters. It was all more complicated than she had supposed.

"After you marry this boy?"

Judy smiled. "Maybe I'll want a girl once in a while. I wouldn't be the first married woman who ever climbed the fence. Husbands would be surprised if they knew what goes on while they're at work."

Erika knew it would never be like that for her. She could never go to bed with a man again—not even for the sake of having children. For that matter, she wasn't sure she wanted children, although she knew that all women were supposed to. She had stopped being a child, herself, on a cold day in her thirteenth year. And since then she hadn't known many children.

She laid a palm against her flat belly and tried to imagine a baby growing in there. It was impossible.

Nor could she imagine herself going from bed to bed as Judy's words suggested, no matter how hungry she was for the excitement and the wonderful rich fulfillment. She wanted one person, only one.

She was suddenly conscious of Judy sitting close beside her, all that smooth young flesh barely covered by the thin housecoat. The valley between Judy's breasts showed shadowy in the light from the dressing-table lamps; the striped material fell away from the soft inside of her thigh.

But passion wasn't the only thing she wanted. There were other things between two people. She was not sure what they were, but even the shocking and wonderful revelation of the night with Peg had been lacking something. Whatever it was, she wanted it all. There was a kindness and a communication that could make love more than just physical; she felt sure of it.

Judy was looking at her under half-closed lids. "How do you feel now?"

"I am all right."

"Feel like playing? Having fun?"

"Please?" But she knew what Judy meant. She felt her face grow hot.

Judy put an inquiring hand on her breast. It felt good. Then it felt exciting. The nipple rose and stiffened to the touch; her back arched involuntarily. A queer ache began to gather in the place that had so recently been invaded and hurt. She didn't know whether it was a good feeling or a bad one. She was afraid and hopeful at the same time.

Judy asked, "Do you like better doing things or having someone do them to you?" As if she were offering a choice between spinach and string beans, like a waitress.

Erika said, afraid yet compelled, "I would like to try—to make you happy."

Judy smiled. She had a rich full-lipped smile that was full of promise. She lay down on the bed beside Erika and slowly untied the belt of her housecoat. The material fell back. There was nothing under it but her body, young and silky-smooth, slender but generously curved, deeply tanned except for two narrow strips of white. Across her breasts with their taut pink buds and across her hips, she looked more naked than anyone Erika had ever seen.

She said huskily, "Erika?"

"Oh, yes. Yes."

She was no longer tired. She knew what she wanted. Not the passive pleasure she had enjoyed at first with Peg, but a chance to stir Judy to flooding excitement.

She put a hand on one rich, round breast, and was excited by the instant response. And bent to kiss Judy on the mouth, not roughly, like a man, but in tender coaxing.

She saw now what she hadn't realized before, that it would be easier with the same kind. You know what a girl likes and wants, she thought in a moment of clarity before feeling took over. You know what you want, how you feel about things, so you can understand another woman. It's like making love to yourself, only better.

She stroked Judy's shoulder, feeling no urgency. Judy said in a whisper, "That's right. We have all night." She gave Erika a peculiarly beautiful smile.

Now she was glad for the night in Peg's bed, no matter how much suffering it had precipitated her into. She was grateful to Peg for teaching her all the things she had to know in order to make Judy happy.

Judy took her hand and moved it. "Here," she said tensely. "Now. My darling."

CHAPTER TWELVE

SCHOOL OPENED the day after Labor Day, the first Tuesday in September. It was exciting, confusing, and terrifying. Erika spent the first day going from room to room, pushed along by crowds of yelling and laughing young people, so nervous she forgot most of her English and was unable to understand directions when she asked for and got them. She was afraid of getting lost, and of being laughed at. If they laugh, she thought, I will go away and never come back.

And how was she to keep up with these others, who not only spoke a slangy language not to be found in books but also felt at home in a hubbub? They knew where they were going and what to expect when they got there. They knew one another. She shrank back into a corner of the first-floor corridor and let them go by, until the last bell sounded. Then, miraculously, the halls emptied and no one was left except a worried-looking teacher who bore down upon her. "Where are you supposed to be?"

Erika held out her course card.

"Oh, this is your study period. Well, classes are only fifteen minutes today. Wait and go to the next one. It's Room 100, right down the hall." And she was gone, a stack of notebooks under her arm, a frown on her forehead.

There was no one in the girls' washroom. Erika looked critically at herself in the long mirror over the row of hand basins. She had dressed carefully for this important day, putting on the dress Mrs. Miller had selected for her, a pink and white striped cotton

79

with a full skirt and a ruffle at the neck. It felt cumbersome after the weeks in shorts. And she looked thin, pale, and hungry alongside these self-possessed girls who had always belonged.

No one could like me, she thought sadly. Not even Judy, who was getting ready to go back to the university; she would live in a dormitory from Monday through Friday, coming home on weekends. Judy had been kind to her, but kindness wasn't what she wanted.

And Judy had given her some bad moments since the night of their first coming together. She wanted to be made love to when she wanted it, imperiously, and not to be bothered merely because Erika was in the mood. It had its compensations but Erika was afraid of being rebuffed, and the first refusal still rankled.

She got out her new lipstick, which matched the dress, and applied a thick layer. It felt oily. She wiped most of it off with a tissue and mentally classed makeup with fancy dresses: too much bother, all right for other people.

Her last class was over at three-fifteen. She followed the other students out through the imposing front doors, then was afraid she had left her locker open and went back to see, making her way against a stream of youngsters all headed for home. But no, the lock was closed, and the card with the combination was in the new notebook with her first assignments. She hugged it to her as she left for the second time.

Out in the sunshine, boys and girls stood around in little chummy groups, talking. In a fenced field across the street four girls in green gym rompers were practicing basketball shots. She crossed the street and stood beside the high wire fence, looking not at the girls but at the impressive facade of the high school building. It covered almost a city block. She didn't think she would ever be able to find her way around in it.

A girl walking past said, "Hi." Erika turned, startled. But she was already half a block away.

She sighed and started home. Maybe Judy would be in a friendly mood. Even without physical contact, she would have welcomed some companionship.

Judy was in the patio with four other girls, college students Erika had seen before and vaguely recognized. They were smoking and drinking pop, sprawled over the outdoor furniture with a lot of bare leg showing. Erika swallowed hard, looking at them through the kitchen window. It was impossible not to notice the bodies of girls when they went around with so few clothes on, bosoms half bare, thighs exposed, underarms tender and vulnerable.

Peg came out of the house and sat down on the arm of Judy's chair, their legs touching, her bare arm thrown across the frame behind Judy's shoulders. She looked pleased with herself.

Mrs. Miller came into the kitchen, carrying a large sack of groceries and jingling the car keys. "How was school?"

Erika hurried to take the sack from her. "Too large. I was lost once."

"You'll get used to it. Everything's large here." The twinkle in her eyes reminded Erika that she, too, was an American by adoption. "Were people nice to you?"

"Yes, thank you, but I forgot my English."

"It'll be easier tomorrow," Lucy Miller promised. She looked tired, the lines around her eyes deeper than usual. "How many of those girls do you suppose will stay to supper? Besides Peg, of course." She peered out of the window. "Maybe I'll just make cheeseburgers and a bowl of salad."

"Do you have everything you need?"

"I think so. Thank you, dear. You're a real help to me."

At least I can be useful in the kitchen, Erika thought. She went upstairs to change the pink and white dress for shorts and a knit shirt, wondering if Peg would stay. And if she did, would she spend the night with Judy?

That I cannot bear, Erika thought miserable. The idea of Peg and Judy in the big double bed, while she lay awake wondering what was happening on the other side of the wall—worse, knowing what was happening, because it had also happened to her. She sighed.

"Will you girls stay for supper? I'll have everything ready in a few minutes."

"Oh, thank you, Missus Miller, but my mother expects me home. My grandmother and grandfather are coming over."

Politely, sweetly, they made their excuses and left. All but Peg, who seemed to take for granted that she would stay. She seated herself at Mr. Miller's right hand with the air of a member of the family.

They had such pretty manners, Erika thought. They were so courteous to older people. She had read about American teenagers in Miss Campbell's magazines. They were rude and destructive and immoral and even, sometimes, criminal. What were these girls like, then, away from home, with no parents around? Did they drink too much? Did they make love with boys in parked cars? She couldn't reconcile what she had read and heard with what she was seeing.

She sat across the table from Peg, spreading pickle relish on her sandwich—Mrs. Miller had made hamburgers after all, they were the easiest thing—and trying not to look at either of the other girls. Was Peg's left hand on Judy's leg, under the tablecloth?

What were they thinking and planning behind those polite blank faces?

But I, too, look calm, she reminded herself, taking a long swallow of cold milk. It means nothing.

Peg asked her, "How was high school?"

"Very large and full of noises."

"You'll get used to it in no time."

Judy made no comment. She sat erect, eating daintily. Erika looked in vain for any sign of the tenderness or passion she remembered on that shut face. She felt locked out and apprehensive.

Carl Miller got up to serve the ice cream that was dessert almost every night in this hot weather. "What are you girls doing tonight?" His glasses shone with good will.

Judy said flatly, "Nothing. Junior wanted me to go to the passion pit and see a double feature, but it's too hot to be mauled around. Besides, I don't like sci-fi and that's all he ever wants to see."

"Me either," Peg agreed.

"Erika, how about you?"

Erika said, "I have many large books to study, and also I must press a dress for tomorrow."

"You need to get out more. Have some fun."

She made herself smile. Mrs. Miller said, "She'll be making friends now that school has started."

She couldn't manage the smile, though, while the older girls rushed through the dishes together, refusing her help, and then went upstairs "to fix their faces." She sat at the dining table, cleared for study, and looked through her new books. They were full of unfamiliar words, and in her fatigue and depression the print seemed to blur. I will never be able to do it, she thought. But she couldn't keep her mind on schoolwork. She thought about Judy and Peg. What were they doing up there?

They came down combed and bright with new

lipstick. "We're going to the drugstore. We'll be right back."

"Why don't you take Erika with you?"

"Sure, come along."

"No, thank you."

"Oh, go with the girls."

Erika shook her head.

Judy said, "Oh, come on." It was a command, bright and hard. Her eyes were insistent. Erika stood up slowly. "All right. But I must study when I come back."

Judy said, "Nobody does any homework the first week." She pushed the younger girl through the door ahead of her.

Erika didn't know what to say, since the other two walked along in silence. She stayed close to the edge of the sidewalk, smelling the freshness of the cut grass and clover from watered lawns. They passed a vacant lot grown tall with burdocks and plantain, a path worn across one corner by children's feet. Peg said, "Gosh, this town bores me. I'd like to live in New York or somewhere."

"Maybe I'll get a job in Paris after my Junior Year. Do you suppose I could, or do you have to be French?"

Erika's heart sank. Peg said seriously, "I don't think Paris is like it was in the Twenties. It's all commercial now."

"Gee, thanks. That's encouraging."

"Anyhow, you have to come back and get your degree. Your father would flip, you alone on the Left Bank."

Erika looked from one to the other, trying to understand. Judy was going away in a year—less than a year, the school term was only nine months. And she would be left alone, without anyone.

The drugstore was crowded. Every booth was full.

The girls wandered around looking at costume jewelry, nail polish and eye liner, paperback books on the racks. They would buy something they didn't really want, she knew, to justify wasting their time this way. The place was full of people buying things for something to do.

Sure enough, they came out with two magazines and a jar of cream shampoo. Judy asked, as if it didn't matter one way or the other, "You coming home with us?"

"Not tonight. Why don't you come home with me?"

"No, I have some things to do."

They stood looking at each other. Then Peg smiled. "Okay. See you tomorrow, maybe."

"We'll walk you home."

"Don't bother." She was gone, walking with her long, easy stride, not looking back.

Erika was confused. She felt glad that Peg had gone home alone, and uneasy about school, and afraid of Judy. The expression on Judy's face was the one she dreaded most, cool and impersonal. It was a look that could cover anger.

But she didn't make a scene. They walked home quickly, Erika hurrying a little to keep up. These girls all had such long legs, and they never seemed to be tired. Judy might be bitchy at the breakfast table after coming in at three o'clock, but she could go swimming if someone called before she finished her coffee.

It is the orange juice, Erika thought wisely, remembering her starved childhood. And the hamburgers and good roast beef, and fried chicken and salads and always milk to drink. A country where everyone has enough to eat—it's wonderful.

She had said so, bashfully, to Carl Miller. His answer baffled her. "I'll take you on a guided tour of Skid Row some day."

She was falling behind. She lengthened her step to catch up to Judy.

Judy stopped on the front porch, a hand on Erika's sleeve—peremptory, not caressing. "Come upstairs. I want to talk to you."

Erika followed her, silently apprehensive.

Judy shut the bedroom door behind them, and turned the latch. "What gives with you and Peg? Are you still sniffing around her?"

"Ich denke nur—"

"Speak English, will you?"

"I am only thinking, maybe you like her best."

"Oh geezus! All this love, love, love all the time! The great big passion of a lifetime! Can't anybody just have fun any more?"

Erika said slowly, "There is more than fun." How could she describe the tenderness that filled her when her hands traveled over Judy's responsive body, her joy when Judy opened all the secrets of passion to her? Fun was a poor enough word for it.

Judy said angrily, "I won't have you snooping around in my private life. You understand me? I don't have to answer to you for anything I do." She looked sulky and mean. "After all, I'm in college. I have friends of my own and I go out with boys—men," she corrected herself. "I can't sit around the house twenty-four hours a day and hold your hand. You haven't any right to expect it."

Erika was silent.

Judy said, "Goddam it, why do you do this to me? I can't even have a friend here without you looking abused. I could be mean to you about Peg," Judy said. "She was the one who brought you out. The minute my back was turned, and you let her do it. Some girls would beat the living hell out of you for that."

"But you had never—"

86

"Makes no difference. If you cared about me at all you'd have waited for me to come home."

"If you cared about me, you would not have her in your room. The day you came home from camp."

Judy's hand shot out. The slap was so unexpected Erika didn't feel it for a moment. Then the blood rushed to her cheek and the skin began to smart.

She said slowly, remembering, "At Steinhagen they hit us on the mouth. Teeth came out, sometimes."

"Oh, my poor baby!" Tears came to Judy's eyes. She gathered Erika to her with muscle-straining vigor. "Do you love me any more?"

"You know I do."

Judy reached for the front of her blouse and began to unbutton it, with shaking fingers that kept slipping off the buttons. "Then love me. Right here. Never mind the bed, just show me if you love me."

She pulled Erika down to the floor, and held her with fingers that hurt. "Now. Quick, right away!"

CHAPTER THIRTEEN

Two WEEKS later they were still making love and fighting and making up again. Not just quarrelling, but fighting. Across Erika's back, under the thin shoulder blades that still stuck out like wings, she wore a row of bruises where Judy had pinched her because she was half an hour late getting home from school.

"I won't have you hanging around with boys after school. They only want one thing from a girl."

"But the English teacher was telling me about some books. Besides, you are often not here when I come in."

"So I'm not here when you come in." Mocking. "The hell with that. You be here when I want you, hear? Or maybe I'll give you a good hard kick where it'll do the most good."

Erika was standing with her back to the dressing-table mirror, peering over her shoulder to inspect the black and blue spots. She whirled around to face the taller girl. "Then maybe I give you one, too. I have had all the beatings I need."

"Oh hell, I wouldn't beat you." Judy came up behind her, put both arms around her and began kissing the bruises. Her lips moved across Erika's shoulders, light and hot and exciting. She said sadly, "Why do you make me act so bitchy?"

Erika said nothing. She stood rigid, sharply aware of each spot where the lips paused and feeling the slow, irresistible rise of need in her body. She didn't want to desire Judy now. She didn't even like her at these moments. But her need was stronger than her anger.

She needed the things they did together, the growing excitement, the quivering thrill that filled her when she brought Judy to tossing, moaning repletion. She couldn't face the world without this secret happiness, marred as it was by dread and resentment.

She shivered. Judy's arms tightened around her. "Love me," she ordered. "Make me happy. Make me!" And added words of her own that Erika had learned were taboo in ordinary talk.

Their lovemaking lasted almost until morning. After Judy fell asleep, heavy-eyed and smiling, Erika lay awake for a long time. She put her head against Judy's shoulder, to find comfort in touching her, and the other girl shrugged it off. Erika moved over to the front of the bed and finally, unable to fall asleep, got up and tiptoed back to her own room.

There is no future in this, she reminded herself sadly, burrowing her head in the pillow. I need to be loved. This little excitement that lasts such a short time—it's not enough.

But it was all she had. It would have to do.

The alarm went off at seven. She got up headachey and silent. Judy was already in the shower. The suitcase at her bedroom door, packed and ready to be carried downstairs, reminded both of them that it was registration day at the university. They looked at each other, but neither smiled.

Judy broke the silence. "Come and wash my back." And when Erika reached for the soap, she held her wrists tightly and pulled her under the cool spray, pajamas and all. They kissed fiercely. Judy said, "I'll be home Friday night. Behave yourself while I'm gone. If I find you playing around with some other chick I'll break your goddam neck. You belong to me."

I belong to myself, Erika thought; but she was afraid to say it.

She sat aimlessly through her morning study period, too tired and depressed to focus on the page in front of her. Her eyes filled with tears when she reflected that Judy was going to be away for five whole days. And at the same time she was unwillingly aware of a feeling of relief. No more rapture and no anxiety, no jealous outbursts, no slaps or pinches. She would be empty, but what a peaceful emptiness!

It could be so good between us, she thought. It comes so close to being good when we make love together. Why can't we talk together at other times, or show some liking for each other? It is as though she hated me.

The buzzer startled her. She gathered up her books and climbed the stairs to her history class, trying to pull herself together. It was impossible to keep up with the assignments even when she kept her mind on it. The language problem and her lack of schooling made a double handicap.

She had asked Mrs. Miller if she couldn't do something easier. Go back to grade school, maybe, and learn with the little children? But it seemed that in America they had something called "social promotion." That meant that even if you were lazy or stupid, you moved through the school system with your age group, emerging with a diploma and no wish ever to open a book again.

"Don't worry about it," Lucy Miller said. "They'll pass you if you are polite and friendly, even if you don't turn in a paper or pass an examination all year. Besides, you're a refugee. You have a special status."

"But I will not know anything!"

Mrs. Miller's voice became very British, with an edge of irony. "No one will care. Judy's not learning

90

anything in college, except how to drink beer and pass true-false tests. Why are you concerned about learning?"

It was so strange, Erika thought as she settled down at the assigned desk and opened her history book. All this education, available to everybody, and no one wanted it. She had already noticed that the pupils who recited well and turned in their papers promptly were the unstylish and unglamorous, the ones who didn't matter in the social life of the high school.

The teacher entered at the back of the room and started briskly toward the raised desk at the front. She stopped, seeing Erika's tear-filled eyes and bowed head. "What's the matter, Erika? *Was ist's mit Ihnen?*"

The tears spilled over. She murmured, "*Ach Gott, Sie sprechen Deutsch?*"

"Only in emergencies," Miss Weber said. She opened her briefcase and brought out a handful of rumpled but clean tissues. "Are you free next period? Good. Stop and see me after class."

Erika gave her a grateful look. She was a tall young woman, maybe thirty, with no makeup and her hair pulled back in a careless bun. Dark skirt, white shirt with sleeves pushed up, hand-stitched loafers. Erika thought she looked like a young mother, but not an American mother.

She sat through the next fifty minutes thinking not about the Louisiana Purchase and the political changes it brought about, nor even about Judy, but about the teacher's pleasant voice and calm expression. In a way she was like Miss Campbell. At least, Erika thought, you could see what she looked like without mentally wiping off the pancake makeup, lipstick, eye shadow and five or six other kinds of expensive scented makeup. It was a nice change.

Today it took the other pupils a long time to filter out of the room. Some stopped to ask about a test they were expecting; others, to hand in late papers. When they were all gone Erika dared to raise her eyes to the teacher's desk. Miss Weber got up, smoothing her skirt. She walked rapidly down the aisle and wedged her long legs under the desk across from Erika's. "Now, what's the trouble?"

I cannot tell her all, Erika reminded herself. Both Peg and Judy had warned her to keep their secret. But the other, the lessons—that was all right to talk about. She chose her words carefully. "My English is too bad. I do not know what the lessons mean. Better I should go in a school with the little ones and learn from the beginning, then I know something when I finish."

"I think so too."

"But they have the social promotion."

"Oh. Modern educational theory," Miss Weber said, sounding not unlike Mrs. Miller. "How about a tutor?"

The word was new to Erika. "Please?"

"A teacher. Somebody who would help you after school or in the evening, until your vocabulary improved so you could keep up with the others."

Erika nodded. "Yes, that will be good. But I have no money for paying such a teacher." She blushed. "I cannot ask the Millers. They are so kind already —no one else has ever been so kind."

Miss Weber said slowly, "I'll do it free if you'll really work. An evening every week. You could come to my place for lessons, if the Millers are willing."

"Thank you." She felt dazed. Things were happening too fast. "May I speak with Missus Miller about this?"

"Sure, see what she thinks. I'm free every night but Tuesday. Choir practice on Tuesdays."

"Please?"

"I play the organ for the people who sing in church," the teacher explained, choosing her words carefully and watching Erika's face for any sign of bewilderment. "Do you sing? You have a good speaking voice."

Erika's smile was bitter. I have had so much to sing about since I was twelve years old, she thought. But that was one of the things she was supposed to forget. She said, "When I was a small child I had piano lessons, but I have forgotten all."

"It would come back if you started again. But I suppose you'd better stick to English and history for a while." Miss Weber gave her a friendly pat on the shoulder. "Come on, I'll walk as far as the corner with you."

Erika was halfway home, full of happy excitement, before she remembered that Judy wouldn't be there.

Mrs. Miller, appealed to while they washed the supper dishes together, was pleased. "It's a wonderful idea. I was going to offer to help with your homework, but I've never taught on a high-school level. You'll learn faster this way. What do you think, Carl?"

"We could pay her, if it comes to that." Carl Miller leaned against the doorframe. "There's no better investment than a young person who wants to learn."

Erika shook her head. "I think she likes better to do it for nothing." She didn't know how she knew, but she felt that making money wasn't in the teacher's plan.

She knew, too, that it wasn't only book learning she needed but a magic formula for belonging. She wanted to be like the casual, secure girls who sat around the patio with Judy. And for all her wanting, she felt fairly sure she would never make it.

But nothing could make her feel depressed tonight.

At bedtime she glanced in at the open door of Judy's room and saw in its orderly emptiness only the promise of Judy's return on Friday night; only four days to wait, and they would be full of new promises. She wanted to write and tell Judy about it, hoping for a sharing that was too seldom forthcoming in their sweet and stormy relationship. But Judy would think that was foolish. Might even be angry about it.

She undressed, went to bed and lay awake for all of five minutes, trying to force her attention away from the exciting prospect of having lessons so that she could miss Judy. She had looked forward to a sentimental night of lying awake and thinking about Judy, the softness of her bosom and the anguished sounds she made in her moments of fulfillment. But before she got that far in remembering, she was asleep.

Thursday would be a good evening, Miss Weber agreed the next day. She was glad that the Millers favored her plan. Erika wondered if she ought to bring up the question of money. Finally she decided that Mr. Miller could approach the teacher on the matter if he wanted to. After all, it was his money.

She asked shyly, "Why do you do this thing?"

"Well, I like to teach." Miss Weber looked away as if this were some kind of sentimentality and she ought to be ashamed of it. "And besides—"

Erika asked, "What is besides?"

"You look like someone I used to know. All right, I'll see you Thursday about eight. Tell Missus Miller I'll see that you get home all right."

Carl Miller said that was no problem, he would pick her up at ten, or she could take a taxi. "No need for your teacher to go to all that bother. Be sure and take cab fare."

"I will walk home."

94

"No. It's not as bad here as in the city, but some messy things have been known to happen here. Sluggings and purse-snatchings."

Miss Weber's apartment was the third floor of a remodelled white frame residence, with a private entrance. Erika rang the bell and waited, hearing the accelerated beating of her heart. A buzzer sounded. She shoved the door open, remembering her terror the first time she had heard an electric door-opener; she had gone calling with Mrs. Miller, and had supposed it was a signal for police or guards. Now she knew better, but she felt for the sound the same unreasoning terror that self-operated elevators aroused in her. She tried to look calm as she shut the door behind her.

The sound of music filled the stair well. Rich and deep, made up of many complex interlocking sounds, it woke an echo from her almost-forgotten childhood. Sunday afternoon, and Vati and Mutti with other grownups sitting on velvet chairs, while she listened from a footstool—where and when? She stood still, listening. Then a voice called, "Come on up," and she ran lightly up the two long flights of carpeted stairs.

The door at the top was open. Miss Weber, in tailored slacks and a plaid shirt, was sitting on a low chair, cigarette in hand. She smiled at Erika and motioned at the sofa, which was covered with a South American blanket in jagged white and black designs. Erika tiptoed in and sat down, running her fingers nervously over the woolly, rather harsh surface of the blanket. The music filled and overflowed the room; it was calm, but it commanded attention. She didn't even wonder where it came from until it stopped, with a tiny click that shocked her after the final resolving chord. Miss Weber got up and lifted the needle from the record, and she saw that the top shelf of the long bookcase held the uncased components of a radio and record player.

"Bach. Toccata and Fugue in D Minor. Like it?"

She nodded, unable to say that she needed to hear it again, to make some meaning out of all that harmony.

"Want a cold drink? You're too young for beer, aren't you? Come and see my kitchen, and I'll check the refrigerator."

Erika followed her obediently into the tiny kitchen, which was bright with a blue linoleum and yellow cafe curtains, bright yellow dishes piled on the shelves of the built-in cupboards. The stove was about a third as big as Mrs. Miller's, which still scared her with all its buttons and different burners; she had refused to learn to cook because she was afraid of what would happen if she pushed the wrong switch. But it would be fun to keep house here. She said bashfully, "It is a nice kitchen. Do you live alone here?"

Miss Weber was bent over, reaching into the junior-size refrigerator, her face hidden. She said, "Yes. I used to share an apartment with a friend, but she moved out." Her tone warned Erika not to ask any more questions.

They took their glasses into the living room, passing a closed door on the way. "Bathroom, if you want to wash your hands or anything." A second door stood open, showing a neat single bed and small chest of drawers. Miss Weber led the way to the front room, removed a pile of papers from the desk and put them on the floor, with a dictionary to weight them down. She carried two straight chairs across the room. "What did you bring? Good. I'll start with history, that's clear in my head from today's classes. You're not planning to be a history teacher, I hope."

"I do not plan yet. Everything is too fast."

"It's too fast for most of us." She sounded like Mrs. Miller, Erika thought. Maybe older people understood things better than Judy and her friends, Erika thought. But how do you make friends with them? She said aloud, "Maybe I am an older person myself."

"Now what do you mean by that?"

"I am not sure."

"Then let it go."

Erika looked at her. "I think I would like to do something that has music in it. Music makes one so free."

It was a new idea. She hadn't given any real thought to the future, in all the excitement and change. But she would have to earn her living, and not only because she had no family. In America most people seemed to work for a living, and a very good one too, with big cars and electric stoves. Now she was surprised to find her thoughts centered around music.

But why not? she asked herself. Other people do it. There are music teachers at the high school, three of them; one for singing and one for the band and orchestra, and one who teaches people to listen. She said, "One could teach music in a school *nicht?*"

"One could. You wouldn't get rich at it, but I can think of worse ways to make a living."

She thought about it at intervals during the next two hours, while she tried to keep her mind on Miss Weber's explanation of the westward expansion and, later, of the difference between adverbs and adjectives. Finally she decided to weigh all the pros and cons later, in bed. That was a good place for thinking as well as some other things.

The teacher walked down two flights of stairs with her at ten, while the Yellow Cab waited. At the door she stopped. "You really might teach, you know. Try

97

listening to music every chance you get, and see how you feel by the time you're ready to make out your college course. Of course you'll go to college—there are work plans and scholarships."

College! She hadn't thought beyond the first six weeks of high school, the period for which report cards would be issued. Now the future was opening up for years to come.

It was the first real attempt at planning. She wondered about it all the way home, whether to be happy or frightened.

CHAPTER FOURTEEN

JUDY'S FIRST evening at home, after a week away, was a bitter letdown. She breezed in with a suitcase full of laundry as her mother was serving the Friday evening meal, showered, and went out again with one of the young men she dated from time to time. The long evening without her was a torment to Erika, who had been waiting since Monday to see her. She kept looking at the clock while she helped Mrs. Miller with the dishes and tried to concentrate on her homework, but its hands seemed to be stuck. Weeks and years crawled past before it was ten o'clock and she could go to bed without having anyone ask if she didn't feel well.

She tiptoed into Judy's room. She didn't want to snoop, but she felt compelled to look for some sign that Judy was still herself, something that would reassure her. Judy had thrown three words in her direction from the front door as she left: "Hi, how's school?" As if I were six years old, Erika thought. She shivered, although the September night was hot.

It was hard to believe that she had ever embraced a Judy stripped and writhing in passion; that her hands and mouth had known the secret places of that beautiful, indifferent young body. Had she, perhaps, dreamed the whole thing? In the camp when it was very cold and the soup was thinner than usual, she had spent whole days with her eyes shut, pretending that Mutti and little Kurt were still alive and she was a child at home again. There had been confused moments when she couldn't separate reality from daydreaming. Maybe she had dreamed the affair with Judy?

But no, that was impossible. I didn't know about it, she reminded herself. You don't just make up such a thing.

She looked around Judy's room, which in the half-hour between her homecoming and departure had taken on the look of a disaster area. Drawers stood open, clothes lay on the floor, caps were off the little jars and bottles that cluttered the dressing table. A damp towel trailed across the Hollywood bed and metal curlers were scattered over the spread. She moved to pick them up, and tripped over a narrow high-heeled linen pump that lay on its side near the door. She picked it up and held it to her cheek, smiling. Judy had beautiful feet—and she curled her toes when she was sexually excited.

No, what she remembered was definitely no dream. There was a pink cashmere sweater on the floor beside the second slipper. She picked that up too, fondling its silky softness. The name tape inside the neck said Dorothy Armour.

So who is Dorothy Armour? she asked herself, and got no answer. She felt a little sick, as she had when a balding middle-aged officer hit her in the stomach because he was impotent. What is a Dorothy Armour doing in this room?

She knew that Judy and her friends wore each other's clothes, keeping them in constant circulation; the high school girls did, too. They had no feelings about sharing their possessions. But she dropped the sweater as though it were red-hot, and wiped her burning palms down the sides of her shorts. Automatically, she lined up the linen pumps under the edge of the bed before she tiptoed out of the room and shut the door on all the things that belonged to Judy.

She was still awake when the car stopped in front of the house, a little after two o'clock. She went to the window and knelt down, elbows on the sill, so she could see under the edge of the shade. It was a convertible, and the top was down. In the moonlight she could see Judy and her date in each other's arms. They sat wrapped together, kissing, for a long time. Then the boy put his hand down the front of Judy's party dress, and she snuggled closer to him. Erika felt violently ill.

Will they? No, not in public. But maybe they already have, and this is the last act? She shivered.

Erika peered closer. It was hard to tell at this distance, from above and in the fading light of the setting moon, just what was happening. The two in the car huddled together. She hoped they wouldn't put up the top for greater privacy.

After a long time Judy got out of the car. She stumbled a little, and the boy put out his hand to steady her. She kissed him, leaning over at a precarious angle for a girl who had evidently had too much to drink. Then she walked unevenly to the house, and the car drove away.

Erika got stiffly to her feet. She crawled into bed, feeling the bottom sheet hot and wrinkled from four hours of sleepless tossing. The pillow was lumpy under her head. Her skin felt tender and sensitive, as though she were coming down with something. And she wanted to cry. For what? She wasn't sure.

She rolled over on her side and listened while the front door opened and slammed shut again, and the sound of high heels began irregularly to climb the stairs.

She's been drinking, Erika thought. She wished Judy would think to take off her shoes before their clatter woke her mother. But Judy was on some other wave length. She got to the top of the stairs and stood there for a moment, muttering under her breath, and then went into the bathroom. Then there was a sharp crash and Judy said, "Oh, damn," loudly. Drinking glass, Erika thought, imagining splinters all over the tiled floor and in the fuzz of the bath mat.

Judy picked her way to her own room. The door creaked.

Erika sat up. Her pajamas were soaked with sweat. She peeled them off, running her hands over her damp body and noticing that she had filled out, these last weeks. Her chest was no longer flat and she was slim, not bony. Her skin glimmered white in the moonlight as she stepped into the hall.

Judy lay on her bed fully dressed, her feet dangling over the side. Erika took off her sandals and arranged them alongside the linen pumps under the edge of the bed. The flowered ballet-length formal was crushed and wrinkled, a long stain down the front. She wondered if she could get it off, or at least unzipped, without waking Judy.

But Judy's eyes were open. She said fuzzily, "Whassa matta?"

"You are sleeping in your dress."

Judy giggled. "You look all right without yours. Looks sorta nice. Come here."

She reached up and pulled Erika down beside her. "Put your hand right here," she commanded, pulling back her skirt and the crinoline petticoat with it. Under the full skirts she was naked. The white moonlight glimmered on her long shapely legs.

Erika began to shake, although the night was sultry. She laid her cheek against the other girl. Judy said in a voice full of sudden urgency, "Make love to me. Right now—hurry!"

But this wasn't the way she wanted it, Erika thought with a flicker of rebellion. She wanted to hold Judy tenderly against her, feeling the need begin

102

and grow in both of them. She wanted to hold Judy's firm solid breasts in her hands and feel their weight and softness, feel the nipples grow hard and proud under her searching lips. Love should be a slow thing, a take-your-time thing that pleased two people equally. Judy moved restlessly. "What's the matter? What are we waiting for?"

The scene in the convertible was still printed on Erika's mind. She said soberly, "I saw you with him."

"So what?"

"He makes you excited, and then you come to me."

Judy's face grew bitter. "Geezus, you don't think I like to have men pawing at me? I can't even stand the way they smell. Dirty lecherous bastards, it makes me sick at my stomach."

"Then why?"

Judy shut her eyes. All her urgency had vanished; her face might have been carved from stone. "You have to go out with boys if you want to be anybody. Otherwise people talk. Just like you have to get married eventually. Gads, that's a happy thought."

"I won't."

Judy laughed unpleasantly. "Wait and see. They'll brainwash you."

"Not everyone marries. Miss Weber at school—"

"A dried-up old maid with no life of her own. That would be great, wouldn't it?" Judy's eyes flew open. She stared into Erika's thoughtful face. "How'd we get into this round table discussion? Don't you like me any more?"

She sat up, pushing the hair back from her forehead. "I'm all wound up in this crazy dress. Take it off for me, huh?"

Erika knew better than to argue when she was in this mood. This was the way she looked when she pinched and slapped and the drinks didn't make it any better. Judy's breath was sour, heavy with stale alcohol and tobacco. Erika turned her face away as she unfastened the little side zipper and pulled the full-skirted dress over Judy's head.

The uplift bra was already unhooked and there was a dark smudge on one lacy cup, as though someone had grasped it with a dirty hand. Erika pulled it off, then bent and gathered the pink bud in her lips as though their wet warm pressure could wash away the male touch.

"Ooh, that's good. I get all excited when you do that. Do the other one, too."

Erika's answer was lost in her helpless need. How could a girl be such a bitch, and then so sweet, all in one second?

She knew the answer. Judy wanted to be excited, titillated, thrilled all through and then lulled to sleep by the caresses Erika knew so well how to provide. No matter what she said or thought, the boy's kisses had disturbed her. Erika was excited, too, by the other girl's nearness. The need to love Judy spread through her body, giving her no choice.

With seeking fingers and then demanding mouth she moved over the other girl's body, stroking the curves and hollows she knew so well, finding the places where her touch made Judy shiver and moan. Judy made a deep sound in the back of her throat. "Make me do it. Please, please."

Erika bent over her waiting body. Judy gasped. "Yes. Yes. Now!"

Erika forgot everything else as the excitement flowed through her body. This is enough, she thought.

But much later, lying awake with Judy's damp satiated body heavy against her, she knew that it wasn't enough. It was wonderful while it lasted, but it wasn't enough.

She wanted someone to like her because she was

Erika, a separate person with needs and ideas of her own. Not just a pair of hands that knew how to excite another woman's body and a mouth skilled in secret caresses.

She stirred, moving away from Judy so that the cool early morning air came between them. It was the first time she had ever wanted to free herself from Judy's touch. Tears stung her eyes at the realization. But she lay for a long time wanting something. She knew it wasn't passion that she lacked, but she couldn't decide what it was.

Kindness, perhaps? She turned her head to look at Judy, who was sleeping deeply, exhausted with dancing and liquor and sex. But there was no answer in that unconscious face, and she didn't know anyone else who could help her find one.

CHAPTER FIFTEEN

"ALL RIGHT, then what's a preposition?"

Erika looked up at Miss Weber's ceiling as if the answer might be printed on the off-white plaster. "A word?" she suggested. Miss Weber grinned. She smiled too, guiltily. "It tells where things are. Over, under, in, on."

"Can you give me some sentences?"

Erika looked at the study lamp. The light blurred around the edge of the brown metal shade. She shook her head. "I am sorry."

Her head ached, and none of the words that crossed her mind seemed to belong together. She rubbed her eyes with the back of her hand. "Please, I will do better on Thursday."

For the first time she felt sorry that the tutoring evenings had expanded to two a week, Monday as well as Thursday. Monday, so filled with memories of the weekend, was no time to meet the teacher's gently asking eyes. Afraid that Miss Weber might read her mind, she sat looking at the cover of her closed book.

"What's the matter, Erika?"

The concern in the older woman's voice was too much for her. Tears spilled out of her eyes and ran down her face. She put up a hand to wipe them off. "Excuse me, please."

"I don't want to snoop, but if you feel like telling me what's wrong, I don't repeat things."

Erika fought with a temptation to pour out the whole story. Shared, her guilt and misery would be easier to live with. But how could she ever tell anyone what had happened on that weekend?

Friday night hadn't been so bad, except for the agony of seeing Judy in a young man's arms. At least she had held Judy, later, and made her happy, even though the experience left her feeling empty and exhausted. Making love was absorbing and wonderful while it was happening, even if there was a letdown afterward. And Judy had gone to sleep satisfied, loving and tender—for a change.

On Saturday morning the fireworks began.

I shouldn't have gone back to my own bed, Erika thought, living it over in memory.

She had left Judy at daybreak, still breathing heavily because of last night's drinks and this morning's spent passion, and had fallen asleep in her own little room. But Judy, getting up to go to the bathroom, had stepped on a piece of broken glass and been jarred fully awake by the pain and blood. And as usual, she blamed Erika. Nothing that happened to Judy was ever her own fault.

She came storming into the little room and woke Erika with a good stinging slap. "Why didn't you stay with me? Now look what I've done!"

"You would have done it anyway."

"I'd have been awake if you were there. Not stumbling around in the dark."

That started the argument. Erika ran out of English as she always did when she was challenged, and sat angry and silent, while Judy swore and scolded and finally, with real tears in her eyes, clawed her neck from chin to collarbone. The long red mark, like the scratch of a cat's claws, was still there under her school blouse. It hurt when she touched it.

What she resented most, however, was her terrible need to make friends again with Judy, even though it meant taking blame she didn't really deserve. She hated herself, yet she couldn't help it. She hung around the house Saturday afternoon, washing Judy's nylons and hanging them on the shower rail, sorting her clothes for the automatic washer, ironing her blouses. She ran gladly to the drugstore for Covermark—Judy had a tiny pimple on her chin. I am like those slaves they had in the old days, she thought as she hurried home through the morning heat. She pushed the damp hair back from her forehead with a sweaty wrist. Mr. Lincoln missed me when he freed the others, she thought wryly, with a little smile.

Mrs. Miller scolded her mildly. "Don't wear yourself out doing Judy's errands. Let her wait on herself. There's no reason for you to do it."

"But there is."

Mrs. Miller was washing the electric mixer. She laid the beaters carefully in the drying rack. "Look here, Erika, you're here because we want you. Like a daughter of our own. Carl feels that way too. You don't have to wait on anyone."

That wasn't the reason she had meant, but she was glad Mrs. Miller misunderstood. She took the little package upstairs to Judy, who was sitting on the bed polishing her toenails. "Thanks. I hope you got the skin-colored kind."

Erika smiled nervously, not having known there was more than one kind. But it was all right. Judy said, "Hand me a tissue, will you?"

She was so beautiful. Even now, looking at her made Erika tingle with desire. In short shorts and a tubular knitted top that left her shoulders bare she was tall and tanned and healthy-looking, like a beauty contest winner advertising milk or vitamins. There were narrow white lines at the edges of her shorts and at the fullest part of her bosom where the soft fabric ended was another white strip. The sight made

Erika long to reach out and run a fingertip along the soft whiteness, then follow it into the hidden places under the garments.

"What are you looking at?"

"Nothing."

"Like it?" A smile curved Judy's lips. She pulled the knitted top down a fraction of an inch. "They're better than Peg's. Hers are like fried eggs."

Erika wanted to look away, but she couldn't. Judy said softly, "Come here."

She didn't know whether she was about to be kissed or slapped. The glint in Judy's eyes could mean either. She moved slowly across the bedroom, still looking at the edge of white along the soft fabric. Judy finished painting her toenails and bent to set the bottle on the floor. Automatically, Erika picked it up and tightened the cap.

Judy's index finger, the nail the same shade as her freshly decorated toenails, reached out and ran along the scratch from chin to breastbone. "Does it hurt?"

She winced. "No."

"I'm sorry, but my head ached. I had too many beers at the party. And it scared me seeing all that blood spout out."

Not only beer, Erika thought, and not only at the party. Besides, Judy was capable of hitting her when she was cold sober. But she kept still.

Judy's finger traveled down her chest and inserted itself in the A-cup bra. "These are getting bigger. Take it off and let me see."

Was she laughing? Erika's cheeks were red, but she unhooked the narrow strip of material and let Judy finger her nipples. They rose to the touch, betraying her by their sensitive urgency. Judy said teasingly, "Do you like that? Does it give you funny feelings?"

She wouldn't answer. But the funny feelings were there, all right. They drowned out her anger and threatened to sweep away the last traces of her resentment against Judy. She had been unfair. And vicious. All right—but there was this hunger.

Judy's smile widened. "All right, then I'll do something nice for you. Or wait a minute, we'll both do it. Like you did with Peg."

"How do you know?"

"I know Peg." Judy pulled her down on the bed, one arm still around her, the fingers covering her throbbing breast. "Never mind Peg. Help me take off these silly shorts."

So then it was wonderful again, after all the misery. They made mutual love on the unmade bed, on top of all the blouses Erika had ironed so carefully, in the hot summer sunshine. Nothing mattered but the wild feeling that swept them both away.

And then on Saturday night, and Sunday afternoon, and again on Sunday night Judy went out with the same young man who had taken her to the dance on Friday. He would take her back to the dormitory after the Sunday evening cookout, he said cheerfully, throwing her suitcase into the convertible. And they were gone, Judy in a beach outfit designed to produce an instant anatomical reaction in any young man who got close to her. Erika went to bed and lay suffering over the thought of Judy on a dark beach, outside the flickering light of the campfire, with a man's hands exploring the curves of that suit.

She woke up with a bursting headache and a feeling of relief that Judy would be out of the house for another five days.

Now, in Miss Weber's little apartment, she kept her face turned away as though the teacher might read her thoughts. "It's nothing."

"It's none of my business," Miss Weber admitted, "but sometimes things aren't as bad as they seem.

110

Not that I think you're in the habit of exaggeration, but there may be answers you haven't thought about. Is it a boy?"

Erika stared at her. "Is what a boy? Oh, no, no! I do not know any boys. Only in my classes."

"Well then, is it because you don't know a boy?"

A dim smile shone through Erika's tears. "No, there is really nothing wrong."

"You're just crying for fun? All right, that's your story and you can stick to it if you want to."

For one more moment she was tempted. What a relief it would be to tell this kind woman everything, to spill all her guilts and ask for advice! She looked longingly at Miss Weber, whose gaze was fixed on her face with gentle concern and something else she couldn't name. Tenderness, maybe?

She shook her head. It was impossible to describe the things she and Judy did together. Even if Peg and Judy had not impressed upon her the necessity for secrecy, she didn't know acceptable words for it. And if she told it would be the end of everything. The Millers might even turn her out. She would be lost.

And it would be terrible for Peg and Judy. How could she hide the identity of her partners in guilt? They were the only ones she knew well enough.

She forced herself to smile. It felt wrong on her face, but it was the best she could do. "Nothing is wrong. I am sorry to have this headache, it makes me forget my words. Please, can we do the prepositions again? This time I try to do better."

111

CHAPTER SIXTEEN

It wasn't easy to do better. Sometimes she felt that it had been simpler in the camp. You endured cold and hunger and the ever-present dread of torture and death because there was nothing else to do. Life was bad, sometimes even worse than the prospect of dying, but some perversity made you hang on to it even if you didn't have anything to look forward to. There were no complications; it was a matter of dogged endurance.

Here everything was complex even for a girl of sixteen. You were constantly being asked to decide things; adult matters you weren't really qualified to cope with. It was scary.

For example, Mrs. Miller kept asking her why she didn't bring some of the girls home. "After school some day for coke and cookies. Or Sunday night supper. Boys too of course, but you'll make friends with the girls first, I hope."

"I do not know anyone."

"Then it's time you got acquainted, dear. Make friends among the girls, then you'll get along all right with the boys."

But I do not want to get along with the boys, Erika thought. She said, "It is not so easy. Everyone already belongs to a little group. Some are important, the ones who have their names always in the school paper—others not. I don't know how to begin."

"With someone else who's new, perhaps?" Mrs. Miller's forehead puckered as it did in the super-market when she was confronted with more than two kinds of Sunday roast. "Not just anyone, of course, but someone you think you might like."

That still didn't help. Mrs. Miller must have realized it, because she started out in another direction. "Go out for some activity. Debating or the paper—no, I suppose not, your English is still a little sketchy. There must be something." She reflected Erika's grin. "How about basketball?"

"We do it in the gym class, but when I throw the ball it never goes in the right place."

"Well, it will work out. I wish Judy were still in high school and could take you under her wing."

That's all I need, Erika thought. Judy eyeing every girl as a potential rival, and slapping her if she said good morning to one of them. Or on the other hand, Judy flirting with her classmates while she writhed in jealousy. It was bad enough to think of Judy at college, sharing a room with the Dorothy Armour who owned the pink cashmere sweater. Who knew what went on at night after the two girls were undressed and the lights out? She was glad she hadn't met Dorothy; knowing was worse than wondering.

She decided it was a good thing to have Judy out of the house and out of her life five days a week, even if she never became part of a high school crowd. She was beginning to learn something about history, grammar, and the mysterious algebra, even if the rules of basketball didn't make sense. And she found herself answering questions without making a quick translation first.

"I have decided what to do when I am old enough," she told Miss Weber. They had gone briskly through two hours of question and answer, a recorded Bach partita and several cups of black coffee. Erika was developing a taste for classical music and coffee at the same time.

113

"At your age I wanted to be a trapeze performer in a circus." The little creases around the teacher's eyes deepened when she smiled. "What's your ambition?"

"Please, I'm serious. I want to be a teacher of music."

"Better get busy, then. You're pretty old for a beginner. You should have had eight or nine years of lessons by this time."

Erika sighed. Miss Weber patted her shoulder lightly. "We'll add some Elementary Principles of Music to these sessions. Language won't matter so much—the terms are all Italian anyway," she added with a laugh. "You'll have to play the piano fairly well and you really ought to have one other instrument, if you plan to earn your living as a teacher. Get in all the listening you can, too. I don't mean rock-and-roll either."

Well, Erika thought, that would also be complicated, but at least she could follow directions. Lessons were easy once you could understand what the words meant. You read a certain number of pages and did the assigned exercises. It was a good satisfying feeling to close the books after an evening of homework; she couldn't understand the girls who bragged that they hadn't cracked a book since September.

Surprisingly, Judy was all for the music lessons. "Sure, you'll never get rich teaching, but it's a steady job with a pension at the end of it. And a foreign accent won't hurt. You talk better all the time anyhow," she added generously. "Make Dad get the piano tuned. They haven't had it done in years."

This was the Judy that Erika had first met and fallen in love with—the friendly, kind camp counsellor. If it could be this way all the time! It would almost be worth while getting along without physical love to have Judy this friendly.

Almost, but not quite.

She did think, though, that she could get along without having her hair pulled and her neck scratched.

The teasing was even worse.

"Come here, baby." That was Judy, stretched out on her bed in the shortest and thinnest of gowns, smiling and purring like a kitten. "Put your hand on me, right here. Mmm, that's the way, angel child."

Until the excitement was more than she could bear and she ached to pull off the thin gown and feel the full length of Judy's body against her, skin to skin. To hold Judy in her arms, like twin parts of a single unit. Wistfully, "I love you so much."

Judy yawned, turning her back. "Gosh, I'm sleepy." Pulling up her knees so that the twin globes of her round and inviting behind strained against the thin fabric. "I'm sorry, honey. You better sleep in your own bed tonight."

But she wasn't sorry, she was enjoying it. Her eyes sparkled with malice and her lips curved in a wicked smile. She hid her face in the pillow so Erika couldn't even kiss her good-night. There was nothing to do but go back to her own room and lie awake, aching with her need, looking open-eyed into the darkness.

Almost as bad were the weekends when Judy was cool and polite, avoiding her, giving her no chance to start anything. Then they sat across the table from each other at mealtime and washed dishes together or Judy might even invite her to the Honey Bee for a malt, to sit in a booth under the eyes of twenty high-school boys and girls. She could see the sweet passionate curve of Judy's mouth and the proud line of her bosom and the way her thigh muscles flowed and flexed when she crossed her knees, and it was like having a sheet of glass between herself and everything desirable.

At these times Judy slept with her bedroom door shut. Erika wasn't brave enough to see if it was locked, since Judy was quite capable of hitting her if she pushed in. She did lock the bathroom door. Erika, in the hall, could visualize the sleek curves under the downpour of water, the lift of her breasts as she reached for the towel. It was maddening.

With Judy out of the house, she could keep her mind on other things for hours at a time.

Especially music. She was spending an extra hour with Miss Weber, every Saturday afternoon, studying the theory of music and demonstrating what she had practiced on the Miller upright (tuned, as Judy had suggested). The teacher never seemed to be too busy or tired for her. And every day she hurried home after her last class, not minding the way the others stood around in little gossipping groups. She didn't have friends, but the keyboard was waiting for her and every day she made progress. It was like working out problems in algebra, but more fun.

"I know I am not a musician," she explained. The teacher nodded. "That's a relief. Most young people who are willing to work think they're Mozart or Beethoven, and when they learn the facts of life they give up. You don't have to be a genius. Just be a good worker."

"If I can learn to be a teacher—you see, I must earn my living. Now I am living on the kindness of other people."

Miss Weber laughed. "Nothing to it, if you can resist the urge to get married at eighteen and have a flock of babies right away."

"I will never marry."

"You may change your mind."

"Why? You are not married."

"Well, that's different." There was a sadness in Miss Weber's expression that made Erika wish she hadn't said anything. She said, "I'm sorry. I was not polite."

"That's all right. Now for next time practice your exercises, and we'll start working on some real music."

For the first time she wondered why the teacher hadn't married. Maybe she loved someone and he died in the war, she thought. Or maybe, but no, that is not possible. But she decided she would watch carefully for some indication of where Miss Weber's interests lay.

Having Judy around on weekends was a series of problems lightened by unpredictable but hoped-for pleasures. On the other hand, the music was a daily pleasure complicated by problems. Nothing was perfect. But at least, Erika thought, her weekday problems had answers, if she could find them. There was no solution for the disappointments and hurts of her relationship with Judy.

Summer was over. Leaves turned brown and orange and red, and drifted off the branches. In the comfortable suburb of Worthington they were raked and piled along the edge of the street, and burned. In years to come the blue and bitter smoke of burning leaves would always remind Erika of her first American October. The high school band practices "The Stars and Stripes Forever" through all her morning study periods; on the football practice fields numbers rang out and heavy bodies ran and thudded together; groups of young girls walked along at noon, gay in sweaters and pleated skirts. The shop windows were full of winter clothes even though the thermometer registered in the eighties, many afternoons.

Mrs. Miller took Erika shopping for cold weather school clothes, and she discovered that the big department stores didn't frighten her any more. She chose her sweaters and hand-stitched loafers critically. Like the food and the language, the abundance in the store had become something to take for granted. She was becoming an American.

But she still had no friends. And the sight of Judy undressing, dropping her clothes carelessly on the floor and standing naked under the electric light, could make her forget everything else. Even the music had no value compared with Judy's touch. On Fridays she had a hard time keeping her mind on lessons; her heart thumped and her throat tightened when she realized that Judy might come to her bed that night.

She had no doubt that she loved Judy. But she wondered sometimes, unwillingly, if she liked her. How could you like someone who might slap you without warning, or kiss you until your head was spinning and then send you away ravenous for more?

By this time the corridors of Worthington High, so terrifying a few weeks earlier, were as familiar to her as the palm of her own hand. She walked from class to class with her books in her arms, looking at girls. Was one of them, secretly, a girl who could give her the kind of love she needed?

She knew it was too much to ask. Even if such a girl existed among her schoolmates, how could she identify her? But she kept on looking.

CHAPTER SEVENTEEN

The assembly buzzer broke into the last notes of "God Bless America." Erika gathered up her notebooks and walked out of the auditorium through a tumult of voices and banging theater-type seats. A curly-haired boy bumped into her, muttered an apology and rushed away. She didn't even hear him.

I do not understand, she thought. This is a public school. We are still almost children—fourteen, fifteen. At least, she corrected herself, the others are children. Her own childhood was so far in the past that she could hardly remember it; so much had happened, and anyway at sixteen she was older than most of her classmates. If she wasn't ready for a competitive social life, how could they be? She knew about things the existence of which they had not even suspected.

She pushed into the back of her mind all the things she could never share with these sheltered adolescents. There was no way to tell them, even if she had wanted to.

A hand touched her shoulder. She turned. Miss Weber smiled at her. "Did I scare you? Where are you going in such a hurry?"

Erika blinked. "Study hall, I think. Yes."

"What's the matter, someone sing off key in Freshman Assembly?"

She knew it was a joke, but she didn't feel like smiling. "I do not understand something. Is it really a dance for the Freshmen, and are boys asking girls to go with them? In school?"

"The Thanksgiving Hop, sure. They have it every year. But they have it in a hotel ballroom, I believe."

"But school is for learning."

Miss Weber said dryly, "And flirting and football games and dressing like everyone else. I don't know if that's bad or good. Both, maybe. Depends on what you want out of life."

"I do not want dances with boys."

"I suppose not. Well, there's no law compelling you to go." The teacher gave her shoulder a pat. "Go on to your study hall. I'll see you this evening."

Maybe she can explain, Erika thought. Because there were too many things she couldn't understand about this strange new world.

But that evening her two hours of tutoring ended in an orgy of listening to new records, and she got off the bus at her corner before she remembered that she hadn't mentioned the dance. I will ask Judy, she thought as she walked briskly home, knowing that the Millers would be watching for her. At least, I will ask her if she seems friendly.

Because you never knew with Judy. She was three girls in one, and Erika never knew which of the trio would get off the bus on Friday evening. There was the friendly big sister of their first meeting, the camp counsellor and Sunday school teacher. There was the Judy she dreaded, cool and courteous when older people were around, blazing with sudden anger if you offered a caress when she wasn't in the mood for it. It was better to stay away from her, or keep other people between you for a shock absorber, if you suspected she was in her dark temper. The trouble was, she could change in a moment, without warning.

Then there was the third Judy, who made all the waiting and even the fights worth while. This was a girl who took you in her arms and held you, teasing and tender, until your whole body was on fire for her. The girl who dropped her clothes on the bedroom floor and stood white as birch bark in the moonlight, waiting to be taken; the wild crazy lover who squirmed and twisted and made little inarticulate sobbing and moaning noises in the back of her throat when you made love to her, until you were both carried away on a high tide of passion. Holding her close after the excitement ebbed, waking at night to find their naked bodies close as stacked plates, Erika was sure this made up for all the rest.

Between times she was not so certain.

She sighed. It had been almost five weeks since she had been allowed to kiss Judy, even. The last time she had begged, and it was a mistake; Judy had been cold and unresponsive as if propositioned by a stranger. Then, when Erika tried to put her arms around the other girl, she got a good hard slap with tennis and swimming muscles behind it; for a moment the room swung around and she nearly fell. Then Judy pushed her out into the hall and slammed the door behind her, and Erika spent the next couple of hours putting wet washcloths on her cheek so Mrs. Miller wouldn't see the red place and ask questions.

Sometimes she wondered how the Millers could help knowing what Judy was really like. She finally decided that parents never know about their children, no matter how bright they are. They don't want to know. They read about all kinds of terrible things in the papers, sex clubs and drug addiction and gang fights, but they never think their own offspring can be involved in anything really evil. And it was true that Judy was always sweet and thoughtful when older people were around. She could afford to be. She got everything she wanted without putting up a struggle.

Erika turned restlessly in bed, wishing she could go away from this house which was becoming more and more like a comfortable prison. I don't belong here, she thought. She didn't know where she belonged, but she intended to find out as soon as she was old enough.

Luckily, Judy was in her camp counsellor mood the next evening. She came in smiling, carried her laundry to the basement herself, and made telephone calls until dinner was ready. If there wasn't going to be any lovemaking this weekend, at least it looked as though there might be no violence. Although, Erika reminded herself, you never knew.

She went into the matter of the dance while they were doing dishes. It made a nice scene, little sister asking advice from big sister. Like the deodorant ads. Erika grinned. Judy sprinkled cleanser on the steak platter. "What's so funny?"

"Really not anything. Judy, did you know that my class at school is going to have a dance? With boys taking girls?"

"Sure. Has somebody invited you?"

"No. But I do not understand. Does everyone go? Is it like classes?"

Judy leaned against the sink. "Heck no. In theory, anyone can go but usually it's only the ones that are in the swim, the girls who date a lot and take part in things. The boys go stag sometimes, but girls don't go to dances without an escort."

"Oh. Then it's all right. I stay away."

She stopped, because Judy was looking at her in a calculating way.

"It might be a good idea for you to go. You don't want to be a drip, do you? A square? Pretty soon the kids will forget you're a foreigner and you'll have to act like everybody else. You know how it is in high school—either you count or you don't. You might as well get in with the right bunch in the beginning."

"But Judy!"

"But Judy what?"

"I do not know any boys."

Judy waved her hand. "That's no problem. The kids in your class are too young and too short, a bunch of shrimps—boys are always about two years behind the same age. What you need is an upper classman." She lit a cigarette and flipped the match into the step-on garbage can. "Peg has a cousin who's, I think, a junior. He doesn't go steady, he plays the field—chances are he'll be free on a Tuesday night. Football man, might get to play in the Thanksgiving game. Big stuff." She smiled maternally at Erika. "Don't worry about a thing. I'll fix it up with Peg."

Erika was speechless. Judy added, "Mother loves to buy clothes, she'll have a ball picking out your first formal. Make her get a ballet length, it's all they wear now."

Erika ignored that. The novelty of new clothes had worn off and she was interested chiefly in having them clean and comfortable. She said in weak protest, "I don't know how to dance."

"It's easy. I'll teach you."

"Please, I can't."

"Why not? Other people learn."

She didn't mean only the dancing. She didn't want to put on a fancy dress and go to a party with a boy. But there was no use telling Judy this. Judy wouldn't listen. She had been dating since she was twelve years old and she expected everyone else to do the same thing. She said reasonably, "It doesn't take any special skill, or anything. Even if you have two left feet you can get around the floor in time to music."

This was the kind helpful Judy she had been longing for, but she hadn't foreseen these results. She said as firmly as she could, "I don't want to go."

"Don't be silly. You have to live a normal life—you might as well start now. Come on, let's finish up here and I'll show you some basic steps. It's easier than you think."

There was no way out of it. She hung up the dish-towel and followed Judy downstairs to the fun room, where the portable record player was kept.

Judy pulled half a dozen albums out of the cabinet. "You don't want to be an oddball. You have to do the things other people do. Then you can do anything you want on the side and get away with it. See?"

It wasn't a philosophy that appealed to Erika, but she didn't know how to say so. When I find my own place in the world, she decided, I will never tell a lie. She stood in the doorway looking stubborn and miserable.

Judy held out her arms. "Come on, I'll show you how to get around the floor without mashing anyone's feet. You might as well start now—you have to do it some time."

CHAPTER EIGHTEEN

"Is your name Erika? I'm Bruce Hall. My cousin Peg asked me to look you up."

She was startled, but she put the books carefully on her locker shelf before she turned around to look at the boy. "Yes." Flatly, because she didn't know what else to say.

He was a good-looking boy, a head taller than she, crew cut, brown eyes. Most of them were good-looking or at least well built; they had always had enough to eat. She looked at him. He said, "You got a little free time before you have to go home? Coke, or something, at the Bee?"

She knew she ought to smile. She had watched girls talking to boys at their lockers. But her face felt stiff. She said, "Sure," and it didn't sound like her voice.

It wasn't real. She wasn't walking down the main corridor of Worthington High in all the four o'clock confusion with a boy at her side, so close that she had to hold her right arm stiff in order not to brush against him. Pretty soon she would wake up and it would be a school morning. But they were on the front steps and then out on the sidewalk, then going into a booth at the Honey Bee and it was still happening. She tried to listen to what he was saying, but it didn't register.

She had read somewhere that men like women who are good listeners. He kept talking about football, and she kept looking at him with an admiring expression. It seemed to be enough.

The expression on the faces of the four girls in the

next booth convinced her that it was no dream. She suppressed a wild urge to run. Just shove the door open and run, pushing people out of the way, seeing their astonished faces look after her. It was all she could do to sit down in the crowded little booth and smile at him.

The waiter put a glass in front of her. Her hand was shaking. When she picked it up, the ice rattled. She gave Bruce an imploring look, but he was describing the lineup for the big game. "Of course I want the team to win, and I don't want anybody to get hurt, but if they have to throw in a sub I'm first in line. Big deal." His smile was proud; he really did think it was a big deal.

Erika said politely, "That would be wonderful. You have to be a very good player, yes?"

"Oh, so-so. You know we've got a good team this year. We're tied for the conference championship."

She had seen football games in the newsreels, a jumble of meaningless running and assault. From Carl Miller's explanations she knew that there were rules and a pattern, but she didn't know enough to answer this nice boy except in the most general terms. Nor could she tell him that she hadn't planned to go to the Thanksgiving game. It was the high point of his year and he was as pleased as a child by the possibility of being in it. She sat still, with a big fake smile pasted on her face, and he went on talking about the games Worthington had won and lost. Ice melted in their glasses.

The Honey Bee had a long mirror running along the side wall at the right height for a girl to check her makeup and hairdo. Usually Erika avoided looking at her reflection. Now she glanced at it and saw her own face looking like any girl's, the right shade of powder on a small straight nose dusted with summer freckles, shoulder-length blonde hair with just

126

a little wave at the ends, in that year's style. A perfectly good face. No one would ever guess that she was different.

"So what do you think about it?"

He had asked a question, and she hadn't heard. She said, feeling the color wash over neck and face, "I beg your pardon?"

"If you don't already have a date for the Freshman Hop, I'd be honored to be your escort. I know it's kind of short notice, but if you don't have anything else planned, why it would be a pleasure."

She was touched by the nice way he put it and the earnest look on his face. For the first time she realized that he was embarrassed too. She wanted terribly to say no. But Judy would be furious. Going to a dance with this Bruce wouldn't be half as bad as facing Judy's anger, even if he stepped on her feet or (what seemed more likely) she stepped on his. She tried again to smile, and produced a fairly good one this time. "Thank you. That would be nice."

He looked relieved. "Well, then, it's settled. I'll see you before then, around. You want another coke?"

She giggled. "No, I must be going. This is my night for lots of homework. Thank you."

A few hours later she sat on Miss Weber's couch, absently stroking the black and white blanket, telling her all about it. "He asked me what color my dress is so he can send me a corsage. What is a corsage? It sounds like underwear."

"Flowers to wear. That's the usual custom."

"He has to pay for the tickets and the flowers too? But he doesn't even know me."

"He has the pleasure of picking you up, dancing with you and taking you home," Miss Weber said with gentle irony. "Not to mention kissing you good night and anything else he can get you to let him do. Besides, you have to buy a dress and all the trim-

127

mings and have your hair done." She hesitated, then added, "He'll probably borrow the family car. In that case he'll want you to park a while after the dance. They all do."

The double crease between Erika's eyes deepened. "That I cannot do."

"Most girls like it—if they can keep themselves and the boys within reasonable limits. It's the first step toward getting married and having a little house in the suburbs and three beautiful children—and a mortgage."

She didn't know how to answer. The teacher looked at her. "Or doesn't that appeal to you either?"

"Please—no men."

Mrs. Weber crossed her knees in well-pressed slacks. "You're planning to live alone? Most girls don't like that."

"I don't know."

"Or do you like girls?"

Erika's eyes widened. But there was nothing in the older woman's face except friendly interest. She said carefully, "Of course, I like some girls very much."

"That wasn't exactly what I meant." Miss Weber stood up, picked up the crumpled pack she had left on the table and took out the last cigarette. She walked well; in her tailored slacks and short-sleeved shirt her figure was trim but feminine. She is quite good-looking, Erika thought. Nice eyes and a truly beautiful mouth. I like her this way, with her own face.

"Let's see, what did you practice this week?"

Erika's mind was not on the music lesson. She wanted, desperately, to tell this kind woman all the things that bothered her. About Judy and her frustrations and also the wonderful pleasure of loving Judy. About her ungrateful feeling that she was trapped in the hospitable Miller household. She wanted to be told what to do.

But she knew she could never tell anyone.

Besides, Miss Weber wouldn't understand. She would think Erika was an evil girl who would corrupt her schoolmates. Perhaps she would even go to the school authorities with the story.

Suppose she told the Millers, and they turned Erika out. Where would she go? Sixteen, penniless, without friends, in a foreign country (but to her all countries were foreign, she was an exile from Steinhagen). Where would she turn for help?

It was a secret that couldn't be shared.

The teacher said briskly, "Well, come on. I gave you a little piece to learn. Let's hear it."

She opened another pack of cigarettes and sat with it in her fingers, forgotten, looking at the back of Erika's head while she stumbled through the juvenile selection she had been practicing all week. Erika made a series of mistakes, broke off and started over. Her forehead was wrinkled with effort. She said, "I am sorry, let me begin one more time." Miss Weber didn't answer. There was silence in the room.

Erika said again, "I'm sorry." She felt like crying. She blinked the tears away.

"That's all right. Why don't you go home now? You'll do better next time."

She didn't want to go. It was only nine o'clock, and the Millers would ask questions if she came in early. Besides, she wanted to stay in this quiet place where she had listened to so much music. It was more like home than the other house. But the teacher sat looking at the floor, waiting for her to leave. There was nothing to do but get up and go.

She put on her warm jacket and closed the apartment door behind her and went slowly down the stairs. Miss Weber didn't stand at the top of the

129

stairs as she usually did, to say her last good-night. Erika closed the entrance door and went out into the night, weighed down by a heavier burden than any she had carried since coming to America—the guilt and insecurity of her love for Judy and her dread of going to the dance with Bruce Hall.

One short year ago she had supposed that if she ever had enough to eat, she wouldn't ask for anything more. Now she was in the land of plenty, with three big meals a day, a refrigerator full of between-meal snacks and a hamburger or ice cream stand on every other corner, and she was too unhappy to be hungry. It was a fine joke on her. But she couldn't laugh.

I wish I could die, she thought miserably.

A cold wind had risen, with the threat of the winter's first snow. She turned up her collar and stood under the street lamp waiting for the bus that would carry her back to Judy's house.

CHAPTER NINETEEN

"IT's A nice dance, isn't it?"

"Wonderful." Erika didn't know who the other girl was. Maybe they had met around school, but all the girls looked different in their party dresses and extra makeup. She didn't know what else to answer to keep the conversation going.

She found the lipstick in her evening bag, drew the outline of a new mouth over her blurred one and began to fill it in. You can't talk and make up your mouth at the same time.

"Are you here with an upper classman?"

Erika nodded proudly, smiling at her reflection in the mirror. The other girl looked envious. But not for long. She said quickly, "One girl brought a University of Chicago man. But maybe he's related to her or something."

Or maybe they are having a big mad affair, Erika thought with a grin. But she had no practice being catty. She put the lipstick and comb back in the little silver bag and took a last critical look at her image in the mirror. The girl there was a stranger, pretty in a pale green dress with a foam of ruffles around the ballet-length skirt and another around the bosom. The two white gardenias Bruce had brought her shone in her hair. A thin rhinestone necklace borrowed from Judy glittered on her neck. Altogether, she thought smugly, a picture from a magazine. The Junior Miss Goes to a Prom.

She couldn't stand here all night admiring herself, no matter how nervous she was about what was coming next. The dance was over. Little groups of boys and girls were leaving, and the hotel employees were starting to put the rented ballroom in order. She gave the other girl a little smile and left the safe refuge of the washroom.

Bruce came forward to meet her, her new fur-collared coat over his arm. "I was beginning to think you went off with some better-looking fellow," he said.

She decided it was a joke. He was smiling and besides, he didn't really think anyone was better-looking than he was. She slipped into the coat and turned the warm collar up, glad she had taken Judy's advice and not let Mrs. Miller buy her an evening wrap. Evening wraps were for college, or the senior year of high at the very earliest. It seemed there were unwritten rules about these things, although Erika didn't know where to find out about them. Anyway, the other girls were all wearing their best street coats, so she guessed she had done the right thing by taking Judy's advice.

It was cold outside; almost the end of November and no snow yet, unusual for this part of the country, Carl Miller said, but an early-morning chill lay over the quiet streets and the air was growing lighter. Soon it would be dawn. Erika's head ached and her feet were tired, two things she hadn't noticed while she was dancing. She wished she could take off the silver sandals; they were her first really high-heeled shoes and the narrow straps cut into her feet. But she tilted a mechanical smile at Bruce, determining to play her role to the end.

It seemed to her that she had been smiling all night. Now she stopped to think about it, her face was tired too.

She said hopefully, "You will have to sleep a lot today? It is the big football game on Thursday."

"Don't worry. I can get along without sleep three,

132

four nights in a row." He unlocked the car door and held it open with a flourish. "Hop in. We'll go down to the Point for a while and watch the sun come up, shall we? And then come back to town and get some waffles or something. Sound okay to you?"

"Sounds wonderful." But fright was like a knife in her. She couldn't stop herself from asking, "Is it all right?"

"At the Point? Sure, half the kids from here will be there. Besides, it's patrolled. Cops aren't taking any chances on people getting rolled or stabbed in this town, not with a reform administration. You've been reading the Chicago papers."

But boys with knives were not what she had in mind. She settled down beside him, wrapping her coat snugly around her knees. Wishing she were somewhere else. Almost anywhere.

It was about a six-mile drive to the Point, the beach where people like the Millers and their friends went in the summer for family picnics. A dozen cars were already parked in an uneven row along the lakefront, a boy and a girl huddled together in each, or two couples. Bruce drove to the end of the line, about twelve feet from the end car, and turned off the ignition. There was a silence broken only by the lapping of the waves and, far overhead, the droning of a single plane.

"How you doing? Having fun?"

"Yes, thank you."

He draped an arm across her shoulder and pulled her against him, smiling a little. It was done so casually that, as with the young sailor, she felt it would be silly to mind. Still smiling, he kissed her. She turned her face away, but not fast enough to escape the kiss. It missed her mouth and landed on her cheek, his lips warm and urgent against the wind-cooled skin.

She said, "Please don't."

"Relax, relax. I'm not going to do anything you don't want me to. What kind of a guy do you think I am?"

She thought that maybe if she could talk to him, start a conversation, she could keep this handling to a minimum. If he got bored it was all the better —he would want to go home. But she couldn't think of anything to say. She felt unreal and scared and slightly nauseated by his presence and his strangeness.

He put a finger under her chin and tipped her face his way and then kissed her again, on the mouth this time. She tried to protest, but the words were smothered. He held her close to him with one arm, pushing the fur-collared coat back with the other hand, pulling the sleeves off her arms. "You don't need this in here. Good heater."

She took a deep breath, and felt his chest pressing against hers, his skin warm under the good shirt.

He put a hand inside the ruffles at the top of her dress. For a second she was torn between two fears, one real, one silly. That he would touch her bare skin, and that he would discover the foam-rubber padding in her strapless bra. It was a ridiculous thing to think about at a time like this, but she was ashamed of the pretense which Judy and Peg and even Mrs. Miller had urged upon her.

He said in a pleased voice, "Hey, these are pretty nice!" Closing his cold fingers around the nipple, and rubbing gently. He pulled her against his body.

Now the man smell reached her. She was back in the hotel room with the sailor. She was in the camp, in the small room with a single overhead light where prisoners were interrogated, and a man was unbuttoning his uniform while another, grinning, held her arms behind her back. She shuddered.

He pushed down the top of her dress and lifted her one small white breast free from the thin material. "You like to have this played with?"

She was too frightened to answer.

Apparently feeling that he no longer needed to hold her down, he released her and ran his freed hand up over her nylon-covered leg, pushed back the full ruffled skirts and stroked the soft white thigh. His fingers were blunt, masculine, clumsy.

"Please no."

"Don't worry, I'm not going to really do anything, not on a first date. What do you think I am?"

You are a man! A silent cry.

He moved the hand higher, feeling his way to the edge of the panty girdle and then slipping his fingers under the thin elastic; moving carefully, seeking.

She was going to be sick.

She wished desperately that she would faint. Or drop dead. But everything looked larger and brighter than usual, and her skin magnified every touch. The tiny roughness of his fingertips caught on her smooth bosom. The sound of the eaves reached her ears with new intensity.

His left hand found what it was searching for, stopped, and then moved again. Now he was at the secret center of her. His hand dug in, hurting her. He said thickly, "Look, put your hand on me."

She stared. He said, "Go on, put your hand on me. You'll be surprised."

Nothing could be worse than this, she thought in horror. In a way it was worse than if he had forced her—he actually thought she wanted to do this thing! He thought she was enjoying it! She looked at him. His face was flushed with excitement, his mouth was half open and he was breathing hard. He didn't look evil, just stupid and excited.

She said with renewed hope, "Please, I do not want to do this."

"Sure you do. It's the most fun there is."

He took his hand out from under her skirt. For a moment she thought he was going to let her go. Relief poured through her. But then he quickly grabbed her hand, moving it toward him. "Well?" He sounded proud and pleased.

She didn't stop to think. She shoved the car door, which was standing ajar an inch or so, and jumped out. He grabbed at her. His fingernail raked across her cheek as she broke loose.

She landed ankle-deep in soft cold sand, recovered her balance, and broke into a run. The high heels sank at every step, so that she ran flat-footed and hindered.

A yell of laughter broke from one of the other parked cars. She realized that they were not isolated, but within sound and hearing of maybe twenty other people. She hesitated. But she realized that none of them would help her. They were probably all doing what he wanted her to do, more or less.

She didn't know whether or not he was following her. She was afraid to look. It was like the horrible dreams of her childhood, when some angry animal chased her and her feet kept sticking to the ground. She tripped on a beer bottle, managed not to fall, and detoured around a child's plastic pail left from the summer. There were crumpled cigarette packs and sandwich papers strewn around. But she felt as though she were the only living person left in the world.

It seemed forever before she reached the edge of the sand and stepped up on the sidewalk, feeling the concrete smooth and hard under the thin soles of her slippers. A few feet beyond, on the other side of a strip of drying grass, ran a four-lane highway. Cars whizzed past, some of the drivers looking curiously at her. Feeling safer, she took a deep breath and looked back at the parked cars. The sand was vacant.

For the first time she realized what she had done. Bruce would tell. The story would be all over school. The Millers would hear about it. And Judy would be angry.

So what? she thought in a small attempt at bravado. I'll say he attacked me. But she knew that nobody would believe her. Bruce was a nice boy from a good family, not the kind to attack you. (Oh yes? She remembered the probing fingers and shivered. But after all, she reminded herself, he had no way of knowing she didn't want a man to touch her there. Other girls apparently liked it.)

All right, then they would think she was naive, and laugh at her. She could stand being laughed at, as long as nobody knew the real reason.

She began to walk quickly along the sidewalk, wanting to get as far away as possible, wondering what to do. She had no money and no wrap—the new coat and the little silver purse were in Bruce's car. She was out in the November wind in a flimsy dancing dress, with no way to get home. And there were all those stories in the papers, purse-snatchers and rapists and murderers who overtook women alone.

Someone else was coming toward her, a tall man. Her heart almost stopped beating. She made herself look. It was a policeman in full uniform, service revolver at his hip.

"What's the matter? Car break down, or did you have a little fight with your boy friend?"

Erika nodded. The officer looked amused, then stern. "Better get home before you come down with pneumonia. It's no time of night for a young girl

137

to be out alone, with the hoodlums and all. Take a taxi."

"I have no money. I left my bag—and coat too."

"Your boy friend parked down there? You want I should go down and read him the riot act?"

"No, no, he went away. I do not know where he is."

She couldn't face Bruce again. Today or ever.

"Come on then, I'll lend you a dollar. I'm a family man myself."

She walked to the corner with him, hugging herself to keep warm, trying not to let her teeth chatter. "Tell me your name so I can send your money back."

"Rheinhardt, down at headquarters. No rush." A cruising cab drifted around the corner. He stepped to the curb and held up a lordly hand. The driver saw the uniform and sat up straight. "Yessir!"

She gave an address. A bill changed hands. The cab pulled into the second lane.

Erika put her head back against the scratchy upholstery and shut her eyes which smarted with fatigue. Now that the actual danger was over, she was beginning to feel afraid.

She had given, not the Miller address, but that of Miss Weber's apartment. She didn't know why, and she was too tired and confused to care. She sat relaxed with her eyes closed, bouncing a little whenever the taxi hit a bump, waiting to get there and tell Miss Weber all that had happened to her.

CHAPTER TWENTY

MARTHA WEBER was already awake when the taxi stopped in front of her building. She had gone to bed early because she couldn't concentrate on the book she was trying to read—the worried face and tear-filled eyes of the little German girl kept getting between her and the print. Around midnight she crawled out of bed, heated a glass of milk and stood beside the sink drinking it slowly, trying to reason herself into calmness. But it didn't help. She was awake for the duration.

It's been a long time, she thought, sitting up and turning on the little reading lamp at the head of the bed. Almost three years since Carole went straight and left. Vanilla pudding years, the kind that slip down easily and have no special flavor.

Yes, but was that a way to live? A brief interval of peace and contentment, sure; with neither love nor sorrow you could get some work done. But on a long-term basis? She reminded herself that her grandmother had lived well into the eighties, vigorous and clear-minded. She was thirty. Did she want another fifty years of nothing?

The luminous face of her alarm clock was a pale green square reminding her that morning was near. Five-ten. Might as well get up and put on the coffee, she thought, pushing the covers back vigorously and swinging her pajama-clad legs to the floor.

A car stopped under her window. She heard a man's voice, then a girl's. You're imagining things, she scolded herself. But she pulled up the shade and looked out. It was Erika all right, unfamiliar in a fluffy dress. She looked timorously up at the top-floor window, then walked resolutely to the front door.

Miss Weber had her finger on the buzzer before the bell rang. She moved quickly through the living room without bothering to turn on the lights. Erika fell into her arms.

This is what I wanted, Martha thought in spite of herself. She resolutely put her own longing from her mind and forced herself to notice that the girl was breathing hard, her pupils dilated, her face terrified. She said, "Come into the kitchen. I'm going to make you a hot drink. What do you want, tea or hot milk?"

"Milk, please."

The little kitchen was orderly and bright. Erika sat on the high stool, dropping her slippers at last and peeling off her sheer stockings, which were full of runs. "I will never wear high heels again. Or go anywhere with a man. Never!"

"You sound a little confused, but I get the idea." Miss Weber bent to look for a small pan. In striped pajamas, with her hair tousled, she looked like a schoolgirl herself. "What happened?"

"We went to the Point. You know where that is?" Martha nodded. Erika's voice was so low that she had to listen carefully to catch the words. "He did things. He put his hands on me." She indicated where he had put his hands. "Then he wanted me to do—something for him."

"And then?"

"I ran away. My coat is in the car. My purse, too. A policeman gave me money for the taxi."

"Here, drink this." She poured the steaming milk into a handled cup and carried it to Erika. "I'll hold it for you. Slowly."

The milk was good. Even better was the experience of being looked after. Erika said with a sigh, "I am so tired. If I could sleep and sleep—but no, I will have to tell everyone. There will be questions." Her face seemed to shrink. "Judy is at home for the vacation. She will hit me."

She stopped, hearing her own words.

"Oh. Judy hits you."

She was quite good at lying, a necessary skill for one who hopes to survive in prison, but she couldn't lie to this tall, quiet woman. "Sometimes. When I make her angry."

She waited for the question. It didn't come. She answered it anyway, all the suppressed anxiety of the last few weeks tumbling out in a torrent. "Sometimes she wants me to—to do things with her. But when she doesn't, or sometimes even afterward, then she hits me. Or scratches, or bites."

"Mmm. Yes, that figures. How long have you and Judy been doing things together?"

"Since summer."

"And was she the first for you?"

Erika remembered that she wasn't supposed to talk about this. Everyone had impressed that upon her— Katja, Peg, Judy. Well, she thought, I am in trouble already, what difference can it make? She was very tired. The milk had made her even sleepier. She felt that she couldn't go on worrying alone; she had to tell someone, and who else was there?

Miss Weber was standing close beside her. Erika leaned her head against a warm arm, and shut her smarting eyes. "There was Katja, in the camp. And Peg. You know, Judy's friend."

"Peg Mathes?"

"She was the first really. With Katja it was, you know, kissing and things. In a camp all is very public."

"I can see that it might be. Peg Mathes. I'll be

141

damned. I've wondered about half a dozen girls but she never occurred to me."

No matter how hard she tried to stay awake, Erika's eyes were closing. To the letdown and the soothing effect of the hot milk was added the wonderful relief of having shared her secret. The guilt fell away from her. She yawned, like a child who has laid all his troubles in the hands of a grownup.

"Here, you're half asleep. Why don't you stay here and sleep? I'll telephone the Millers later. You'll have enough explaining to do as it is, no coat, no date, and that fool boy will probably make a real thing out of it. There's no point in stumbling in at five A.M."

Erika nodded sleepily. "I like to know. Is is wrong in this country for a girl to protect herself? Are they supposed to do these terrible things?"

"If you listen to the parents and teachers, no. Actually, by their own ideas, girls are supposed to let boys go just so far, and then stop them at the last minute. It must be pretty unpleasant a lot of the time —for the boys, too, poor kids."

"When you were younger, too?"

"That was a little different." Martha Weber closed both arms around her and lifted her off the stool. "Come on, I'll put you to bed. My sheets were clean last night, can you use them?"

More asleep than awake, Erika let the teacher guide her into the bedroom, remove the fluffy dress and crinoline petticoat and the strapless bra. I never want to see any of these clothes again, she thought dimly, feeling cool and free, opening her eyes to see that the strapless had left angry red marks on her skin.

Martha Weber touched the marks, gently. Then she laid her palms against the two small breasts, a light warm touch that lasted only a moment. Erika looked up at her, surprised. But she was already bending to roll down the panty girdle, her face as calm as that of a hospital nurse.

"Here's a pajama top. You don't need the bottom, you're too little. Now hop in bed."

The bed, smoothed and tidied and with a fresh pillowcase to undo the marks of Miss Weber's sleepless night, felt incredibly good. She never wanted to get up, or see anyone. Most of all she didn't want to see Judy.

Judy would never like her again—if liking was what they had, Erika thought. She had made Judy look foolish, and that was inexcusable. The other temper spells had been impulse things, no real reason for them except that Judy felt like hitting or scratching. This was going to be a full-dress performance.

She was shocked to discover that she didn't mind the thought of losing Judy, although she shrank from the prospect of going through all that mess. It would be a relief to have Judy out of her life. Only she wouldn't be, of course. They would be spending weekends under the same roof, forever and ever. At least the rest of this year, she amended, remembering the Junior Year in Paris.

"Need another blanket?"

"No, thank you."

"Erika, did you ever make love with a man?"

The girl considered this, with her eyes shut and the comfort of the bed melting her arms and legs into happy numbness. Could you call it love, what had happened in that brightly lighted little room? Americans used the word when they meant something quite different. "No. But men did things to me—they started when I was twelve, in the camp. Soldiers."

"Maybe it would be different with a nice boy."

Erika forced her eyes open. Miss Weber was standing beside the bed, looking at her. She wore her schoolroom expression—the one she assumed when she was being fair and considering all sides of a question.

Erika said, "Bruce is a nice boy. He did not mean to hurt me. I don't like men, the way they touch me or the way they smell."

"I know what you mean," Martha said softly. "You're not the only one. A lot of women feel the same way, if that's any help."

She stooped and laid her cheek against Erika's. "Go to sleep now. I'll take care of everything."

She was already asleep. She heard the tiny click as the light went off, the sound of Miss Weber's bare feet as she crossed the room, the bedroom door closing. She let herself become nothing.

She recognized the feeling; she remembered it from the long-ago lost time. She had lain in bed like this on winter nights, free from worries, hearing her mother play the piano two floors below and knowing that everything was all right. Comfort and security were in the absolute surrender to sleep.

Then is she my mother? she asked herself, trying to puzzle out the feeling that had swept over her at the touch of the teacher's hands. Yes, and there is something more, too. For a moment she felt again the feather-soft touch of Martha's hands on her bosom, a touch of infinite gentleness.

Then she was really asleep.

CHAPTER TWENTY-ONE

It FELT strange to be walking up the front steps of the Miller home in broad daylight, ten in the morning to be exact, wearing a pale green formal with torn ruffles and a pair of silver sandals with dirt smears on them. And Miss Weber's tweed jacket, which was too long and loose and didn't so much cover up last night's messy finery as emphasize it. Nine hours of sleep, a bath and shampoo and a good breakfast couldn't quite undo the effect of those wilted ruffles.

I will never have another dress with ruffles. She added it to her list of nevers, silently, as she climbed up the front steps and tested the door, finding it, thank goodness, unlocked. It occurred to her that it might be a long time before she had a new dress, period. The Millers might very well throw her out because she had insulted the son of their friends, and then stayed out all night.

Too late, she realized that she had forgotten to find out what Miss Weber had said on the telephone. She didn't have a story ready. There was nothing to do but tell the truth.

Bruce had already been there. Her fur-collared coat lay neatly folded over a chair in the hall and the little silver bag was placed neatly on top of it. There was sand on it, looking forlorn in the bright morning sunshine. She picked up both the coat and bag, automatically, and went through the downstairs rooms. No one was there, and if anyone had been worried about her there was no sign of it. Everything was empty and orderly.

145

It now occurred to her that the situation might not be as grim as she had supposed. Perhaps the Millers would only think she was young and stupid. Having undergone the horrors of war and a prison camp, she could perhaps be forgiven for being timid. Then too, she was a newcomer in the country, one who didn't know all the local customs. Even if you didn't know about the soldiers, that was a perfectly reasonable explanation.

They might even pass it by in silence, as no more than an embarrassing social blunder. Then everything would go on as it had before. Except for Judy.

And the looks at school. And the awareness of something, she didn't quite know what, that now existed between herself and Martha Weber. It had existed for quite a while, she suspected, but breakfast this morning had been her first inkling of it.

Breakfast, late and leisurely because today was the first day of Thanksgiving vacation and there were no classes, had been a silent meal. Not awkwardly silent, more like a meal shared by two old friends who can get along without talking. There was no word about anything personal, and no caress at parting—not even a handshake. Miss Weber had said, "Call me later in the day, if it's convenient," and had shut the door and gone back into the apartment.

Whatever she had told Mrs. Miller on the telephone, it would be different from Bruce's story. She decided, reaching the top of the stairs, that she had better say as little as possible.

Her room was exactly as she had left it the evening before, loafers under the bed, twin sweaters across a chair. As though nothing had happened.

She stripped off the formal and crinoline, now very crumpled, and unfastened the sandals; she had worn them after all, because Miss Weber's shoes were all too big. Her rumpled dress made her feel that she needed another bath. She pulled on a terry robe and slippers, and tiptoed to the bathroom.

Halfway through her shower she heard a car stop in the driveway. Mrs. Miller, home from marketing. She had discovered that motors have individual voices, like people. She felt apprehensive, but she went on soaping and scrubbing. One thing at a time, she reminded herself. You have lived through worse things, Erika Frohmann.

Someone was coming upstairs. The bathroom door opened with such vigor that it banged against the laundry hamper and flew shut on the rebound. Judy stood framed in the doorway, pink-cheeked in leather jacket and a little knit cap with a long green wool pigtail. She looked angrier than Erika had ever seen her.

"I see you decided to come home after all. Must have been quite a party."

Erika bit her lips. I will not fight with her, she resolved. But a quiver of fright began deep down in her and spread, so that her hands shook. She stood looking at Judy.

"What happened? He rape you or something?"

It was an out, but she couldn't take it. "He did things to me. Bad things. I don't let any man do such things!"

"For heaven's sake don't yell. My mother's putting away the groceries downstairs." Judy came into the bathroom and sat down on the stool, looking anxious. "It's hot in here."

She pulled off her cap and jacket and tossed them on top of the hamper. She was wearing a tight black jersey shirt with a low V neck that showed the hollow between her breasts, and black slacks. Against the matted fabric her skin looked smooth and rosy. At any other time the sight would have made Erika's heart beat faster. Now she saw, incredulous at first

147

and then joyful, that it didn't matter. The magic of Judy had evaporated.

But she was embarrassed by her own nakedness. She dried herself hastily, wiping off dabs of soap she hadn't quite rinsed off, and got her arms into the sleeves of the terry robe. She said in a voice that shook, "I better get dressed."

"Sure."

She wanted to be alone. But Judy followed her into the bedroom and shut that door too, quietly. Erika began pulling out drawers, wondering if she could go into the closet to put on her underwear. She decided it would look too silly. After all, girls dressed and undressed in front of each other all the time, it didn't mean anything. But she kept walking around the room, picking up garments and laying them down again, to postpone the moment when she would have to take off the robe.

Judy asked too quietly, "What made you go up to Old Lady Weber's? Why didn't you come here?"

"I wanted someone to talk to."

That was the wrong answer. Judy's eyes narrowed. "Oh. I suppose you spilled everything while you were at it?"

The lie came automatically. "I only told her about Bruce. What he tried to do."

"You're lying!"

"No. Honestly, Judy."

Judy stepped back and looked her over. "I might have known you couldn't be trusted. You told her the whole thing. About me, and Peg, and everything. So she can blab it all over town."

"She wouldn't do that."

"What do you mean she wouldn't do that? She's just the type. Bossy old maid." Judy's voice rose accusingly. "You goddam fool. I knew I couldn't trust you. Now you've really loused things up!"

148

Erika couldn't speak. She shook her head, no.

"Oh, don't be a sap. Of course she'll talk. It's probably the juiciest piece of gossip that ever came her way. You can't ever, ever tell straight people the truth about anything!" She banged her fist on the dressing table to emphasize the "evers," making the jars and boxes jump and rattle. "Oh, you—you fool! Do you have the first idea what you've done?"

Erika said stubbornly, "She won't tell."

"I suppose you know all about it. You're an expert on human nature. How come you two are so chummy anyhow?" She stopped, staring at Erika. "Oh. You've been playing around with her behind my back. Hot damn, Weber of all people!"

"That is not true."

Judy started to laugh, a little hysterically. "Geezus, that's wonderful. Old Poker-Face Weber turns out to be a dike in disguise. Wait till the kids hear about that—she'll never live it down."

"You can't."

"Oh yes I can. I can start a rumor that'll run that dame right out of this town. She'll never get another teaching job in Illinois. You wait and see."

"Judy, no. That is so bad."

Judy smiled. It wasn't a pretty smile. "How is she in bed? Better than I am? Do you do my things for her? Come here and show me what you do to her."

Erika looked around, clutching the front of her robe. There was no way to escape. Judy stood between her and the door. And Judy was bigger and stronger than she was. She stood, hugging her arms to her chest, wishing she were dressed.

Judy said sharply, "Tell me!" She moved closer to Erika, still smiling. Slowly and deliberately, she pulled down the black jersey shirt. The neckline tore. She wore nothing under it. The twin globes spilled out, soft yet firm, tipped with eager rose-color. Erika looked away.

Judy said in a loud clear voice, "Put your hands on me. Here. Feel how nice they are."

Erika stood unmoving and expressionless.

Judy said in a coaxing voice, "Come here and kiss me."

"I don't want to."

Judy's fingers undid her waistband zipper. The tight black slacks dropped over the white of her legs. She rolled down her sheer panties. "Come to bed with me, darling. We'll have fun in bed together. I'll do you too, shall I? We'll do it for each other. Come on."

"Please no."

The smile vanished. Judy's face took on the set look that meant trouble. "Why, you cheap little tramp! After all I've done for you. After all my family's done for you! I'll break your goddam neck!"

Mrs. Miller said quietly, "Judy, that will do."

They both looked at her, with identical expressions of shock. Judy picked up her slacks and held them in front of her. She said, not looking at her mother, "We were just kidding."

"It won't do you any good to lie." Mrs. Miller's face was white, but her voice was steady. She looked at Erika. "Has she made you do things you didn't want to do?"

Here was another easy out. But Erika shook her head. "No. I knew about it before."

Judy said eagerly, "She was the one who told me about it. I never even heard of it before."

"No. I think I always really knew." Her mother sat down on the dressing-table bench, as though her knees wouldn't hold her up any longer.

Judy had pulled up her tight trousers and thrown a towel over her shoulders; dressed, she felt braver. "Psychologists say it's very common for adolescent girls to be attracted to other girls. It's a stage in their development. What's so terrible about it?"

"Judy, I read Freud long before you were born." Mrs. Miller tried to smile. It was a failure. "I wouldn't mind so much if you were really a lesbian—not if I thought you really loved someone, and would make a relationship with some decency and kindness in it. What I can't undertsand is this—this meanness. This bullying."

"You're taking her side, and I'm your own daughter!"

"Being my daughter doesn't keep you from being wrong occasionally."

Judy said defensively, "Well, it was her idea, anyway. She talked me into it."

Mrs. Miller said, rubbing the back of her hand across her eyes, "I tried to bring you up according to the child psychology books. Perhaps if I'd given you a good swift slap the first time you lied to me, you might have turned out better. As big as you are, I'll spank you now if you make any trouble for Erika or her teacher."

She was four inches shorter than her daughter, but Erika, watching, didn't doubt that she could do it if she wanted to.

Judy said sullenly, "I'm of age. You can't push me around."

"In that case you can leave college, leave home and get a job. Your father and I have no further responsibility toward you."

"You're not going to tell daddy?"

"Not if you behave yourself."

"That's blackmail." But there was admiration in her voice. Perhaps it was her first realization that her mother could be as tough as she was. Tougher, Erika thought, seeing Judy's scared expression, because she knows she's right. Maybe if she hadn't been so sweet and kind, Judy would have been a nicer girl.

Mrs. Miller looked at Erika. "I'm sorry about all this. You've gone through enough already, I think. Believe me, we didn't know it would be like this."

"You have been only good to me."

"Erika." She stopped, and started again. "I hope you'll learn to like men. The other way is full of problems. But whatever you are, try to be a good person. I've known a few gay girls who had all the dignity and self-respect in the world." She sighed. "We'll try to do better. I don't know the answer yet, but there has to be some way to straighten all this out."

It was clear to Erika what she must do. She picked up Mrs. Miller's cold hand and pressed a respectful kiss on the back, as she had learned in earliest childhood to kiss the hands of grandmothers and elder aunts. It was her homage. She said, "If I could speak to my friend? She is kind—and truly she doesn't tell things."

Mrs. Miller patted her head. "Of course. Use the extension in our room. And please tell her I'd like to talk to her as soon as she has time."

She held the door open. Erika went out quietly, leaving the mother and daughter together.

CHAPTER TWENTY-TWO

"WE'LL HAVE problems," Martha Weber said. She sat holding her cup, letting the coffee get cold while she listed all the pros and cons of Lucy Miller's plan. "There will be talk. Not about Erika or me, but about you and your family. Are you sure you want to do this thing?"

Mrs. Miller nodded. "It's not really an unusual arrangement, except that some people may feel we are disregarding our obligation to Erika, so soon after bringing her to the States. I haven't seen my family since the war began, you know. My mother died in 'forty-three. Pneumonia. Now that my father is getting old and frail, what could be more natural than for me to make him a visit? He'll be delighted."

"But Judy. And Mister Miller."

"Judy will be quite happy in the dormitory. She has her own friends—at any rate she may as well get used to being away from home, if she's going to Paris next year. Perhaps she can grow up a little." Mrs. Miller's smile was strained. "And Carl is quite willing to put up with the inconveniences of hotel life, so that I may see my father. It's not for a very long time, you know. Not more than three or four months, unless I find Father in a much weaker condition than his letters suggest."

"And when you come back?"

"We'll see what happens." Mrs. Miller pulled up the collar of her heavy coat, which she had been putting on by degrees for the last ten minutes, and looked around for her bag. "We're not abandoning

Erika, you know. Carl will give you a check on the first of the month. We'll talk everything over when I come back."

"That's not necessary. I can manage."

"I feel," Lucy Miller said firmly, "that we owe her something."

Erika said eagerly, "I could get a job. After school and Saturdays. A lot of girls in my class work."

"Not until your English is letter-perfect," Mrs. Miller said, bending to kiss her. She held out her hand to Miss Weber. "You don't know how grateful we are."

Martha Weber said slowly, "Are you sure you understand all the implications of this?"

"I'm not sure I understand anything at all about human nature," Lucy Miller said dryly, "but I know a person of character and intelligence when I see one. I trust you—no matter what develops out of this." She pulled on her gloves and left, walking very erectly with her head high, not looking back.

Martha closed the door. "You know," she said, coming back to the low chair where Erika had sat through the visit, "I don't know exactly what this relationship is going to be. It's too soon to tell."

"I know what I want it to be."

"I'm afraid I have the same idea. But let's not rush things, shall we? You're very young."

"I am not that young."

Martha shook her head. "I'm twice your age—and it's been a long time since I felt this way about anybody. Give me time to get used to it, will you?"

Erika laughed. "Oh, I feel so good! And it will not hurt Missus Miller to go and see her sick old father, or Mister Miller to stay at the hotel for a while. He really lives in his office anyway. It will not hurt Judy to live at school all the time. She can find some girls."

"I'm trying not to dislike Judy."

"I feel so strange about her. She was so dear to me, and now nothing is left. Is it always like that?"

A shadow crossed Martha's face. "No, not always. You two didn't have anything in common except sex, you know. That can be quite exciting for a while, but it wears off. Love needs friendship for a foundation."

"This is why you don't hurry?"

"Sure. This way, if we have anything it will be worth keeping."

"You are a wise woman. Me, I'm lucky."

She would have liked to put her arms around Martha and hold her close. She knew that if she helped things along a little, they would be in bed in a very short time in spite of all the good resolutions. But she knew, too, that Martha was right. There was no hurry. Martha wouldn't change, as Judy had, or stop loving her overnight. If she loved at all, it would last.

"What's on your mind?"

"The same thing that is on your mind. But I think you're right. Oh, I'm a lucky girl!"

"I hope so, I'm sure."

She got up and went to stand behind the teacher, leaning over her and putting both arms around her neck. "I know what I think," she said with her cheek against the top of Martha's head. "I think I love you."

"Tell me that ten years from now, when you're old enough to know how you feel."

"All right, I tell you ten years from now. Then and now, too."

They stood touching. Then Martha turned, slowly. Their lips met for the first time. It was a gentle kiss, full of questioning, but full of promise too.

No one knows the future, Martha thought. For now I'll be satisfied with the present.

Erika thought: This is where I belong. Let it be right, from the beginning.

They stood looking at each other, their fingers intertwined, willing to wait.

Publications of
THE NAIAD PRESS, INC.
P.O. Box 10543 • Tallahassee, FL 32302
Mail orders welcome. Please include 15% postage.

To the Cleveland Station by Carol Anne Douglas. A novel. 192 pp.
ISBN 0-930044-27-4 $6.95

The Nesting Place by Sarah Aldridge. A novel. 224 pp. ISBN
0-930044-26-6 $6.95

This Is Not for You by Jane Rule. A novel. 284 pp.
ISBN 0-930044-25-8 $7.95

Faultline by Sheila Ortiz Taylor. A novel. 140 pp.
ISBN 0-930044-24-X $6.95

The Lesbian in Literature by Barbara Grier. 3rd ed. Foreword by
Maida Tilchen. A comprehensive bibliog. 240 pp.   ind. $7.95
ISBN 0-930044-23-1   inst. $10.00

Anna's Country by Elizabeth Lang. A novel. 208 pp.
ISBN 0-930044-19-3 $6.95

Lesbian Writer: Collected Work of Claudia Scott
edited by Frances Hanckel and Susan Windle. Poetry. 128 pp.
ISBN 0-930044-22-3 $4.50

Prism by Valerie Taylor. A novel. 158 pp.
ISBN 0-930044-18-5 $6.95

Black Lesbians: An Annotated Bibliography compiled by
J R Roberts. Foreword by Barbara Smith. 112 pp.   ind. $5.95
ISBN 0-930044-21-5   inst. $8.00

The Marquise and the Novice by Victoria Ramstetter.
A novel. 108 pp.
ISBN 0-930044-16-9 $4.95

Labiaflowers by Tee A. Corinne. 40 pp. $3.95

Outlander by Jane Rule. Short stories, essays. 207 pp.
ISBN 0-930044-17-7 $6.95

Sapphistry: The Book of Lesbian Sexuality
by Pat Califia. 195 pp.
ISBN 0-930044-14-2 $6.95

(continued on next page)

Lesbian-Feminism in Turn-of-the-Century Germany.
An anthology. Translated and edited by Lillian Faderman and
Brigitte Eriksson. 120 pp.
ISBN 0-930044-13-4 $5.95

The Black and White of It by Ann Allen Shockley.
Short stories. 112 pp.
ISBN 0-930044-15-0 $5.95

At the Sweet Hour of Hand-in-Hand by Renée Vivien.
Translated by Sandia Belgrade. Poetry. xix, 81 pp.
ISBN 0-930044-11-8 $5.50

All True Lovers by Sarah Aldridge. A novel. 292 pp.
ISBN 0-930044-10-X $6.95

A Woman Appeared to Me by Renee Vivien. Translated by
Jeannette H. Foster. A novel. xxxi, 65 pp.
ISBN 0-930044-06-1 $5.00

Lesbiana by Barbara Grier. Book reviews from *The Ladder*.
iv, 309 pp.
ISBN 0-930044-05-3 $5.00

Cytherea's Breath by Sarah Aldridge. A novel. 240 pp.
ISBN 0-930044-02-9 $6.95

Tottie by Sarah Aldridge. A novel. 181 pp.
ISBN 0-930044-01-0 $5.95

The Latecomer by Sarah Aldridge. A novel. 107 pp.
ISBN 0-930044-00-2 $5.00

A VOLUTE BOOK
NAIAD PRESS, INC.
P.O. Box 10543
Tallahassee, Florida 32302

All Naiad Press Books listed in this book can be purchased by
  mail, as well as Valerie Taylor's three titles.

**Journey to Fulfillment, A World without Men and Return to
  Lesbos**
  $3.95 each plus 15% postage and handling—minimum 75¢.

NAME _____

ADDRESS _____

CITY _____ STATE _____ ZIP _____

BOOK(S) _____

_____

        TOTAL ENCLOSED $ _____